AF584499

Praise for *Dark Arts and Crafts*

'What a delight! It's unusual to find books aimed at absolute beginners that can be so thoroughly enjoyed by more experienced practitioners. Don't let the beginner-friendly style fool you. These easy-breezy step-by-step tutorials are based in true, well-researched tradition, leaving you in very good shape if you decide to take your practice further, and off-handedly pointing you in all the right directions to do so. Would that all introductions to magic were so enjoyable and yet so useful! The straight-faced, mischievous humour had me literally roaring with laughter all the way through! Magnificent! Bravo! More like this please!'

Denis Poisson, author of *Hidden Paths* and creator of the *Foolish Fish* YouTube Channel

'In a masterful blend of wit and wisdom, this brilliant book weaves together the strands of history and the arcane, creating the paradoxical fit to be equally enlightening and entertaining. Pure alchemical gold!'

Laetitia Barbier, author of *The Art of Tarot*

Dark Arts & Crafts

13 Spells for Love, Money and Self-Care

affirm press

Tehani Perham is one of Australia's most well-respected witches and experts in eclectic witchcraft. She is the co-owner of Muses of Mystery, Melbourne's go-to store for all things magical, metaphysical and other-worldly. Tehani is an initiated priestess, tarot card reader, reiki and shamanic healer.

Dr Peter Coleman is an author whose first book, *Weekends with Matt*, was published by Affirm Press in 2022. He has a PhD in cultural studies from Monash University, where he also tutored in Eastern Philosophy. After leaving university, he started a career in the not-for-profit sector, where he now works as a consultant. He is also an authorised marriage celebrant and occasional tarot card reader.

CONTENTS

INTRODUCTION

'... a touch of magic in this world obsessed with science'

LISLE VON RHUMAN, *DEATH BECOMES HER*

This is a guide to making magic. Not the kind of magic where a guy with a goatee pulls a rabbit out of a hat or makes the Statue of Liberty disappear. We're talking about the kind of magic practised by ancient Egyptian high priestesses, Italian Renaissance wizards and Siberian witches. The magic of myth and legend. The cool kind of magic.

Fortunately, you don't need to be Merlin, or Cher in *The Witches of Eastwick*, to make magic happen. With a few supplies, some simple instructions and a smattering of supernatural power from beyond, we'll show you how to make magic at home for yourself! Why limit your DIY projects to crochet, decoupage, scrapbooking and woodworking – all great hobbies, btw – when you can also use your crafting time to master the ancient art of enchantment? It'll give you plenty to discuss at your next knitting circle meet-up!

RUSSELL-MORGAN PRINT
U.S. PRINTING CO.
CIN. U.S.A.
3730.

We'll be travelling together through the fascinating, mysterious and often hilarious world of dark arts and crafts. You'll learn to protect yourself from negativity, summon cosmic energies, foretell the future, inspire self-love, spark the flame of romance and step into your power – all while making fabulous stuff at home for fun! Who ever said crafting couldn't be a mystical exploration into arcane forces?

But before we fire up the cauldron, let's take a quick trip back in time …

A brief history of magic

Nobody knows when magic first began. We know it's ancient, but exactly how ancient is anyone's guess. Theories suggest that the 17,000-year-old Lascaux cave paintings in south-western France were a form of magic, so it's safe to say that magic is very, *very* ancient.

You can't really talk about magic as a standalone 'thing' in prehistoric times. Tribal cultures didn't separate the natural from the supernatural. Gods, spirits and unseen forces were always working behind the scenes, making the seasons change, the flowers bloom and the sun rise every morning. In a way, the whole world was magical. (It still is!)

It's also hard to talk about the difference between 'tribal' and 'civilised'. What classes as civilisation largely depends on who's doing the talking. Indigenous Australians have the oldest continuous civilisation in the world, dating back 60,000 years.

Because this book mostly features Western magic, we'll be focusing on that version of history. But there isn't just one story of magic. There are countless stories from across the globe and across time. We invite you to explore as many as you can.

According to the stock-standard definition, civilisation officially kicked off in Mesopotamia around 6000 years ago, followed by the ancient Egyptians around 5000 years ago. As it was for their ancestors, the supernatural was a key part of the Egyptian people's world. It shaped their religion, politics and home lives. Healing charms and protective amulets were a dime a dozen. Magic was in everything, like a broken bottle of glitter.

After the ancient Egyptians came the ancient Greeks. The English word 'magic' comes from the ancient Greek word *magos*, which was used to talk smack about the Persian Zoroastrian priesthood known as *maguš*. We don't have time for a deep dive into the Zoroastrians or why the ancient Greeks were throwing shade at them (drama!), but it's worth highlighting that from the ancient Greeks onwards, there was an increasingly negative attitude towards magic, even though it was still widely practised.

With the rise of Christianity and its spread across Europe there was an upswing in anti-magic sentiment. By the late Middle Ages, many magical practices were banned by the Church. Witchcraft was considered demonic and punishable by death. This led to the 'witch craze' between the 1400s and 1700s, when tens of thousands of people were executed across Europe on charges of witchcraft. Anti-magic sentiment had turned into murderous mass hysteria. Not ideal.

At the same time, magic was undergoing a revival in Renaissance Italy. From the late 15th century to the early 17th century, a form of ceremonial magic known as hermeticism became popular in wealthy and educated circles. Hermeticism combined astrology, alchemy, spirit summoning, ancient Greek philosophy, Jewish mysticism and Christian theology (there was a lot going on). Hermeticism was focused on revealing secret knowledge to gain power and wisdom. This was when people started using the word 'occult', which comes from the Latin word *occultus*, meaning 'hidden from view'.

LE PORTRAIT DE LA VOISIN.
Source de tant de maux maudite creature
Qui par mille poisons destruisoit la Nature,
Si la parque en fillant tes detestable jours
A fait regner la Mort, en prolongeant leur cours,
Vn suplice effroyable et plein d'Ignominie
A sceu trancher le fil de ton énorme vie.
Ant. Coypel sculpsit
Chasteau, ex.

The late 17th century to the early 19th century was the Enlightenment in western Europe. This was a time of reason, philosophy and science. Magic was mostly dismissed as lies and superstition. It stayed on the backburner until the mid-19th century, when the Victorian era saw a big uptick in all things supernatural. Ghosts, mediums and fortune-telling were all the rage. Several occult movements sprang up, the most famous being theosophy and the Hermetic Order of the Golden Dawn. Both were a big deal in the history of modern magic and had a major influence on 20th-century tarot, witchcraft and occultism.

In the 20th century we saw magical movements sprout all over the place: neo-paganism, Wicca, chaos magic … the list goes on. The internet made it easier for people to research magic from history and around the world. Magical traditions mixed and mingled like swingers at a key party.

Interest in the supernatural remains strong today. No matter how much science and technology advances, it seems that we still need a touch of magic in our lives.

MAN
XIX. The SUN
X
III

The dark craft path

The term 'dark arts' was originally used to trash-talk magic by people who thought it was wicked and harmful. But they were full of crap and we don't need to roll with their definition. After all, the word 'dark' can also mean shadowy or secret, as in 'kept in the dark'. Why can't dark arts mean mysterious arts? Doesn't that make as much sense as the original meaning? Screw those anti-magic militants! We're reclaiming dark arts as a declaration of pro-magic pride.

In case the title gave you the wrong idea, this book offers zero spells designed to cause harm. It's a hex-free zone. Our dark arts and crafts are about making your life more fabulous, not making anyone else's life worse.

Names and labels can be a tricky thing when it comes to magic. For example, practitioners of Wicca are known as witches, but you don't need to practise Wicca to call yourself a witch. Pretty much anyone of any gender who practises magic can call themselves a witch. The same is true for magician, wizard and sorcerer. These terms can mean different things to different people.

We'll be referring to magic-makers as dark crafters. It's a nifty, neutral term that works well with the book title! Of course, you don't have to call yourself a dark crafter. You don't have to call yourself anything at all. Just come as you are. Spellcasting is an equal-opportunity lifestyle!

Magic is for everyone but not all forms of magic are free for use. Some magical and spiritual traditions have restricted or closed practices. This means you need to be a member of a community or go through initiations before you can practise them. It's important to be mindful of this, particularly if you're interested in traditions from a different cultural or racial background to your own. It's usually easy to find out if something is in the magical public domain or not.

Just ask someone in the know, or google what you're researching along with the word 'restricted'; nine times out of ten you'll find a Reddit feed teeming with strongly worded advice.

The good news is that our dark crafts are perfect for anyone to make and are based in long-standing magical traditions. We're big believers in keeping spells true to their history and philosophy, even if we like to give them a bit of a makeover.

Speaking of philosophy, there's a touch of theory we need to cover before we can get on with any practical magic. But don't worry – we'll be crafting in no time!

Dark craft theory

Magic has always been grounded in a specific understanding of how the universe works. Fortunately, you don't need to read any dusty books of esoteric wisdom before you can start down the dark-crafting path. Once you're across our three magical lessons and the four elements, you'll be good to go!

Three magical lessons

LESSON 1

Magic recognises the life force in everything

A key magical principle is that everything shares in the same life force. When we say life force, we're not just referring to people, animals and plants (although they're all included). We're talking about the life force in the galaxies, the stars, the clouds, the mountains, the rivers, the wind, the stones, the sand, the screwed-up chocolate bar wrapper at the bottom of your bag. From a magical perspective, the whole universe is alive.

LESSON 2

Magic is the art of working with the life force in everything

When we practise magic, we connect with the life force that's all around us. Magic shows us how to communicate with this life force and channel it to achieve the outcomes we're after. Think of magic as a collab project with the energies of nature.

LESSON 3

Magic is the art of directing our own life force through intention

Every one of us is an embodiment of the life force of the universe. Pretty awesome, right? Magic is about connecting with the life force around us and the life force within us. That's why intention is super-important. Your intention is what directs the flow of your life force. Even if you say all the right things and perform all the right steps, a spell won't come out the way you want if your intention is off. A crappy, half-arsed spell motivated by honest intention is much more likely to pay the bills.

The four elements

In case you're not familiar with pre-Socratic Greek philosophy, or you've never watched an episode of *Captain Planet*, the four elements are air, fire, earth and water.

When we talk about the four elements, we're not just talking about physical realities like the sky, the sun, the soil and the sea. The four elements are the fundamental energies that make up who we are. They are the building blocks of magic. We could say a lot more about the four elements, but ain't nobody got time for that. The following summaries of each element should give you all the information you need for now.

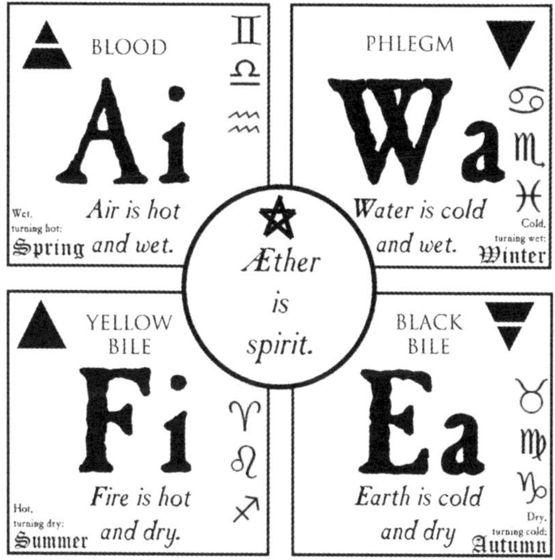

Air

This element is big brain energy. Air represents ideas, new beginnings and imagination. It's all thought but not much action. Picture an absent-minded professor, with glasses and a pencil through her topknot, surrounded by piles of books. When a spell involves smoke, incense or waving a feather around, you're tapping into air energy.

Fire

This element is boss lady energy. Fire represents courage, motivation, taking charge and getting things done. It acts fast and burns bright but can be destructive if left unchecked. Think Meryl Streep's character in *The Devil Wears Prada*. Unsurprisingly, whenever you use candles you harness fire energy … because of the actual fire.

Earth

This element is dirty diva energy. Earth represents grounding, nature and stability. Earth is nurturing but stubborn. Imagine a grandmother who's always there for you and who will do anything to look after you, but who refuses to use a mobile phone. If you're working with salt, stones, flowers or crystals, you're working with earth energy.

Water

This element is major feelings energy. Water represents empathy, healing, creativity and intuition. It's dreamy and sensitive, like an inspirational art teacher who wears pastel linens and regularly cries in front of the class. Receptacles like cauldrons or cups use water energy. Is your cup half-empty or half-full? Whichever way you pour it, you're tapping into a nice flow of energy here.

Keep in mind that magic is about balance. It's important not to focus on the element you're most drawn to, or that best suits your star sign or BuzzFeed personality quiz. Nobody is exclusively connected with one specific element. This isn't Hogwarts and there's no sorting hat. Even if you don't see yourself as a fire person or a water person, those elements are still part of you. You need to draw on all four elements to be the most powerful dark crafter you can be.

That's enough theory for now. Let's get onto the fun part – craft supplies!

Your dark-crafting toolkit

So you've decided to dabble in the dark arts and crafts. Where to begin?

First up, every dark crafter needs their toolkit of must-have items. Fortunately, a good dark crafter will not need a ready supply of chicken's feet, rams' horns or demons' blood. You may need to source some crossroads dirt eventually, but that's easier than you think – just head to your local intersection and dig up some of the nature strip.

Almost everything you'll need can be readily sourced at your local craft store or homewares shop, or can be found in one of those bottom drawers you're too ashamed/embarrassed/terrified to clear out. (Where the hell is Marie Kondo when you need her?) The most 'out there' thing you'll need is a small cauldron – and if you're struggling to get your hands on one of those, a heatproof dish works just as well. Don't overthink it.

The following list doesn't cover everything you'll need for all the crafts in this book, but it does provide an excellent foundation. Once you have all these items, you'll find getting your spells going much easier.

Whenever possible, we recommend recycling, upcycling and using found objects. Not only is it more sustainable, it's also less expensive. Everyone's a winner.

Here is what you'll need:

- ◊ **Burnables:** Burning smelly stuff is a time-honoured magical tradition. We'll cover burnables in more detail in Project 2, but they're primarily used for clearing away negative energies. Sage, palo santo and rosemary are the most popular options.
- ◊ **Candles:** As a dark crafter, you'll find yourself really burning through the candles. Small and medium-sized taper candles are usually the best option. The big thing is to have candles in a wide variety of colours: red, orange, copper, gold, yellow, pink, green, blue, purple, silver, brown, black and white. We recommend you just start stockpiling candles gradually and keep an eye out for any discount coupons at your local candle store.
- ◊ **Cauldron:** When we talk about a cauldron, we're not talking about some massive bowl you stand around in the moonlight with a coven of darkly clad crones (not that there's anything wrong with that – we're all for doubling down on toil and trouble). We're talking about a small cast-iron pot with a lid that you can burn things in. This is one instance where it might be best to shop at a witchcraft store, although camping stores often stock them as well. There's also online shopping.
- ◊ **Crystals and stones:** Many dark crafts require crystals and stones. There are thousands to choose from, but to begin with it's worth picking up a small amethyst, black tourmaline, citrine, clear quartz, hematite, rose quartz, selenite, sunstone and tiger's eye.
- ◊ **Essential oils:** Oils are important for many dark crafts. The most essential essential oils for the crafts in this book are frankincense, ginger, jasmine and rose.

- **Feather:** A feather is mostly used for wafting away smoke after you've done some burning and accidentally tripped the fire alarm. You can use any type of feather you like, but in this case size does matter – the bigger the feather, the better when things get overheated.

- **Glue gun:** It's not the most mystical tool in the world, but a glue gun will always come in handy!

- **Herbs and dried flowers:** Fortunately, many of the condiments you'll need for dark crafting will already be in your pantry. The more esoteric ones can be found online, at witchcraft shops or sometimes at your local health and wellness store. As for dried flowers, we recommend stocking up on rose petals as they always come in handy.

- **Ink:** Many dark crafts involve writing stuff down. Using a biro really doesn't pass the vibe test when it comes to magic. The simplest option is to get yourself a nice fountain pen. If you're really feeling the fantasy, we suggest purchasing a quill and a pot of ink. Be warned, though: using a quill and ink isn't as easy as those period dramas would have you believe.

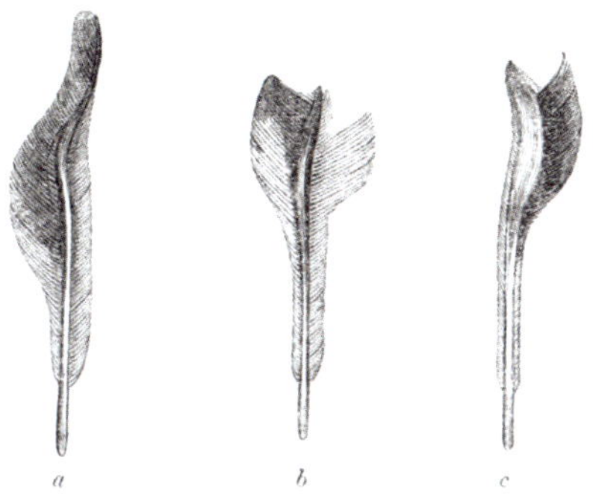

- **Jars:** We suggest you start upcycling every jam jar and condiment pot that comes your way. From performing spells to storing herbs, a dark crafter can never have enough jars.
- **Knife:** Don't stress, we won't be sacrificing any goats. You'll need a knife for carving and chopping inanimate objects. A small kitchen knife will definitely cut it.
- **Matches:** You could also use a cigarette lighter or refillable barbecue torch. You do you.
- **Mortar and pestle:** You need these for grinding up herbs and resins. Using a mortar and pestle also gives a real 'kitchen witch' feel, which is fun.
- **Needle and thread:** Sometimes you gotta sew stuff.
- **Paper:** Sometimes you gotta write stuff down.

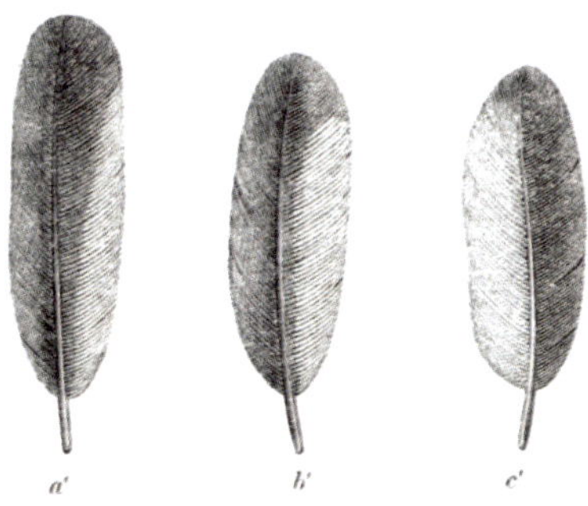

- **Scissors:** Sometimes you gotta snip-snip.
- **Salt:** This stuff isn't just for flavouring food or causing hypertension. Salt has been a spiritual staple for eons, for banishing, cleansing, protecting and purifying. We advise stocking up on the black, Epsom and pink varieties. As with candles and jars, you can never have enough of this magic mineral.
- **Sharpie or permanent marker:** Sometimes you need to go more heavy-duty than a quill and ink pot!
- **Thread and twine:** This is for binding and tying things. (No, not your victims – you're better than that!)

That's the list. We recommend keeping your toolkit all together, either in a box made of alder wood with a pentagram carved into the lid, or in a drawer.

Timing

From the seasonal rituals of the Celtic pagans to the astrological rites of the ancient Mesopotamians, it has long been understood that certain magic should be practised at certain times, either to maximise effectiveness or minimise destructiveness (unless destructiveness is what you're going for …).

For example, according to European folklore, 3am is the witching hour – the time when supernatural activity is most powerful and the veil between worlds grows thin. Shakespeare even alluded to this idea in *Hamlet*:

> *'Tis now the very witching time of night,*
> *When churchyards yawn, and hell itself breathes out*
> *Contagion to this world.*

Don't worry. We're not going to suggest you get up at 3am to complete your dark-crafting projects. And we certainly don't encourage breathing contagion into the world – it's not nice. (We've all had more than enough contagion to deal with in the last few years.)

But we do have a few suggestions for how you might schedule your magical practice, just to give your dark crafting that extra push.

Nördliche Declination der Sonne
FRÜHLING
WINTER
SOMMER
HERBST
Nachtgleichen
Bahn des Merkur
Colur der
Apsiden
Sonne
Linie
Solstitien
Colur der
Bahn der Venus
Südliche Declination der Sonne

The phases of the moon

One of the most popular ways to time dark crafting is according to the phases of the moon. Just as the moon influences the tides, it also influences the power of magic. There are four phases in each lunar cycle. Each phase promotes different qualities you can tap into:

◊ **New moon:** The moon ducks out from behind her curtain and says hello. This phase is all about beginnings and inspiration. This is a time for imagining all the magical things you could do.

◊ **Waxing moon:** The moon is back and looking for attention. This is a great phase for focusing on growth. If you want to start a new dark-crafting project, there's no better time.

◊ **Full moon:** The moon is now at her iconic best – gloves off, no holds barred, performing the half-time show at the Super Bowl. This is a phase for celebration, abundance and fulfilling wishes. Moon magic is at its peak – make it work, designers!

◊ **Waning moon:** The moon goes for after-show drinks and starts to power down. As her light fades, it's a good time to downsize. Maybe unsubscribe from that streaming channel you never watch or break up with your loser boyfriend. Chop-chop, people.

The traditional method for checking the phases of the moon is to look at the sky at night (#lifehack). But who has the time?

Fortunately, there are free lunar cycle apps to help you keep track. If you don't mind splashing some cash, you can also buy a diary or poster that charts the lunar calendar. Nothing quite says 'dark crafter lives here' like a moon phase calendar stuck to the wall.

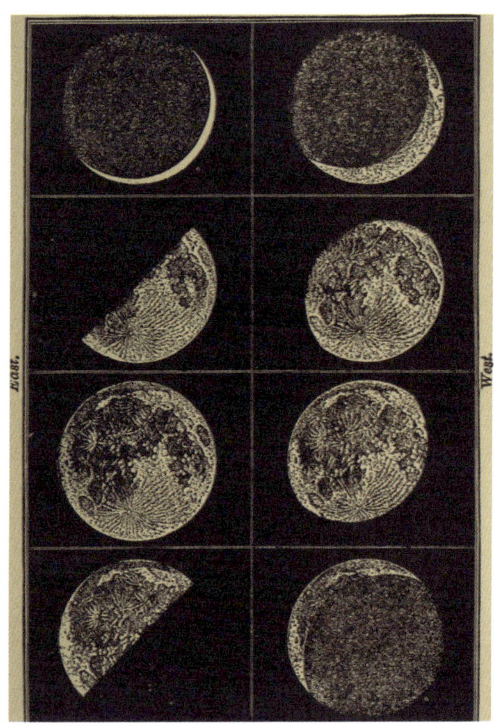

Zwilling
Krebs
leo

Days of the week

In case nobody taught you this in school (and, let's face it, they probably didn't), the days of the week are named after gods and planets. For example, Sunday is named after the sun (bet you didn't see that coming), Friday is named after the Norse goddess Freyja, and Saturday is named after the Roman god Saturn.

Each day of the week is magically connected with the god or planet it is named after. The sun is associated with light and abundance, which makes Sunday the right day for wealth magic. Freyja is the Norse goddess of love and fertility, which makes Friday a great day for love magic.

This reference table will help you work out which day of the week is most appropriate for which kind of dark craft:

DAY OF THE WEEK	ORIGIN OF NAME	ASSOCIATIONS
Sunday	'Sun's Day'	Abundance, success, transformation, desire, action
Monday	'Moon's Day'	Healing, wisdom, intuition, change, flow, emotions
Tuesday	'Tyr's Day'	Conflict, vitality, assertiveness
Wednesday	'Odin's Day'	Business, money, communication, travel, journeys
Thursday	'Thor's Day'	Truth, justice, expansion, knowledge
Friday	'Frejya's Day'	Fertility, sexuality, harmony, love, friendship
Saturday	'Saturn's Day'	Structure, limitations, obstacles, protection, banishment of negativity, death

Planetary hours

If you want to go really hard, consider the planetary hours. This magical system assigns each planetary hour of the day in each day of the week to a particular planet and its associated energies. So, the first planetary hour after sunrise on a Thursday is allocated to Jupiter, and the eighth planetary hour after sunset on a Monday is allocated to Venus.

This is more complicated than you might think, because a planetary hour isn't the same as a regular hour and will vary in length depending on the time between sunrise and sunset on any given day (or between sunset and sunrise on any given night). It's kind of a lot.

If being incredibly detail-oriented is your jam, we suggest doing a deep dive into occult philosophers like Marsilio Ficino and Cornelius Agrippa, who were all about planetary magic. There are charts and diagrams galore for you to explore! But if you're anything like us, remembering to schedule your money magic spell on a Wednesday is hard enough.

Each of the dark crafts in this book has a recommended phase of the moon and day(s) of the week. Please keep in mind that these aren't hard and fast rules. If you can't be bothered with magical timing, don't stress. We totally understand how difficult it is to squeeze spellcasting into a busy modern schedule! Just do your best.

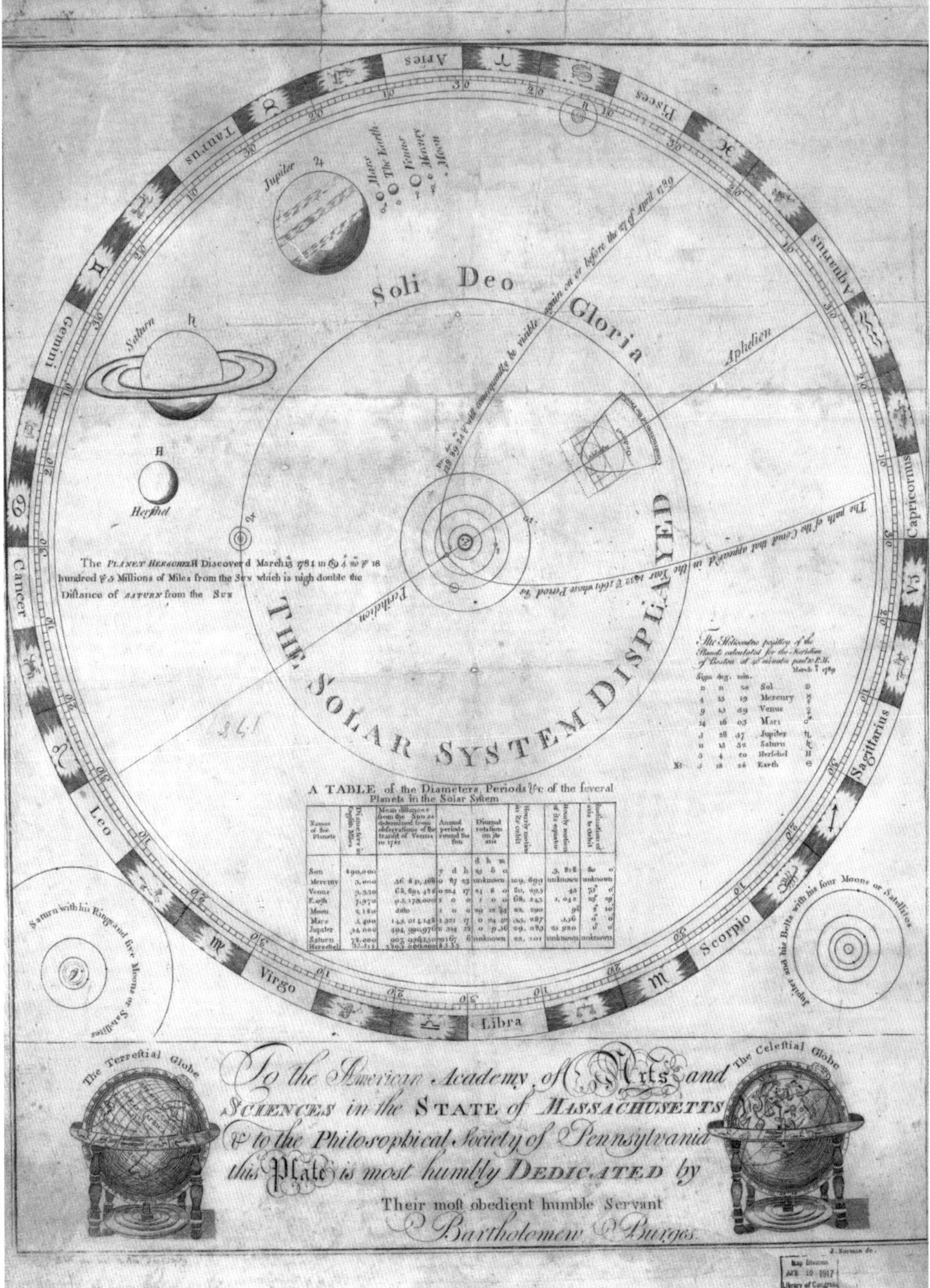

Soli Deo Gloria
THE SOLAR SYSTEM DISPLAYED
Aries
Taurus
Gemini
Cancer
Leo
Virgo
Libra
Scorpio
Sagittarius
Capricornus
Aquarius
Pisces
Jupiter
Mars
The Earth
Venus
Mercury
Moon
Saturn
Herschel
Aphelion
Perihelion
The PLANET HERSCHEL Discoverd March 13 1781 in ♊ 4 20 & 18
hundred & 5 Millions of Miles from the SUN which is nigh double the
Distance of SATURN from the SUN
A TABLE of the Diameters Periods &c of the several Planets in the Solar Sistem
Saturn with his Rings and five Moons or Satellites
Jupiter and his Belts with his four Moons or Satellites
The Terrestial Globe
The Celestial Globe
To the American Academy of Arts and
SCIENCES in the STATE of MASSACHUSETTS
& to the Philosophical Society of Pennsylvania
this Plate is most humbly DEDICATED by
Their most obedient humble Servant
Bartholomew Burges

HEMISPHAERIUM
COELI BOREALE.

Tab. 3.
HEMISPHAERIUM
COELI AUSTRALE.

Your magical roadmap

This book will take you on a guided tour through the fundamentals of the dark craft path. If you're new to magic, we recommend going step by step through each of the projects. This will guarantee you have all the basics covered before you start branching out into any high-powered DIY sorcery. Here's a rundown of the magical landmarks we'll be visiting along the way.

Cleansing and clearing

Before you prepare a nice meal or perform open-heart surgery, it's important to wash your hands. The same principle applies to magic. But instead of cleaning away germs, you have to clean away negativities. Magic works with energy, and you never know what kind of negative energies have taken up residence in your lounge room or built a nest on your left-hand shoulder. It's always important to cleanse and clear before you do your dark crafting. You need to make sure malevolent forces don't get stuck to your glue gun.

Activation

In case you've forgotten in the last ten seconds, magic works with energy. Your power drill and Hello Kitty nightlight need energy to work, and so do your dark crafts. Magical activation is how you plug a spell into the cosmic power source. (Look, it's not exactly like that, but this electricity metaphor is working so let's just stick with it.) There's no point making magic if you don't know how to flick the 'on' switch.

Protection

You know what's better than curing a bad case of foot fungus? Not getting foot fungus at all! Protection magic is the ultimate preventative measure. It's the best way to ensure nasties don't get past your front door in the first place. Think of these dark crafts as metaphysical condoms for your home.

Divination

This is the art of foretelling the future or uncovering hidden knowledge using supernatural methods. It's one of the oldest forms of magic and remains one of the most popular (think of astrology, numerology, tarot cards and so on). We'll be showing you how to make and use your own divination tools. Remember, homemade divination always tastes better than store-bought.

Self-love

Managing our energy is essential for practising dark crafts. Many of us struggle with how we feel about ourselves, and this can have a real impact on our magic, as well as on our general quality of life. That's why self-love is so important. (Before you get yourself too hot and bothered, we're not talking sexual self-love here. That can wait!) We'll teach you dark crafts to spark love and appreciation for the magical wonder that is YOU!

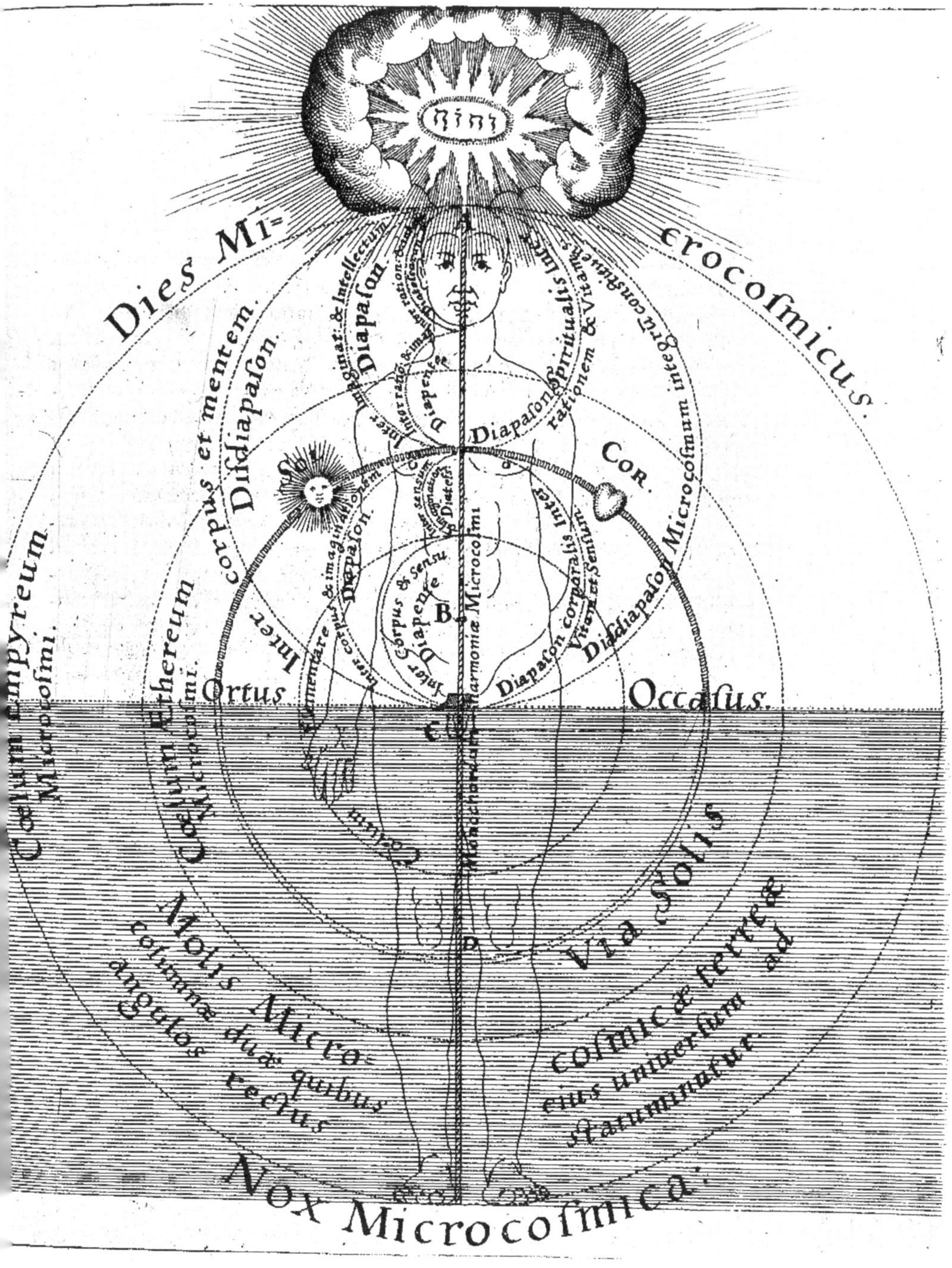

Dies Microcosmicus.

Cœlum Empyreum Microcosmi.

Cœlum Æthereum Microcosmi.

Inter corpus et mentem Disdiapason.

Diapason

Spiritualis lux

Disdiapason

Sol

Cor.

Diapason

Diapente

Inter Corpus & Sensu Diapente

Diapason corporalis lux

Harmoniæ Microcosmi

B.

Ortus

Occasus.

Monochordum

D

Molis Microcosmicæ columnæ duæ quibus anguloś rectus

Via Solis

Nox Microcosmica.

Desire and romance

Once you've ticked off self-love, it's time for other-people-love. Magic has long been used to inspire romance, so why should you miss out? And if you're in the market for something less committed, don't worry – we've got you covered. You'll have gorgeous people dropping into your DMs for some safe and consensual fun in no time!

Confidence and empowerment

The last landmark is about strength and self-belief. You will learn to summon confidence and inspire success. You will celebrate the power that's always been within you. As a final step, you will crown yourself as an accomplished dark crafter and practitioner of the magical arts (cue Beyoncé's 'Flawless'). A fitting end to a fantastic journey!

Along the way, we'll stop at some roadside attractions. These will be fun facts and strange stories from the world of magic and occultism. There's lots to learn and plenty to laugh about.

At the end of the book, you'll find a list of books, podcasts and online resources to help support your ongoing dark-crafting adventure. There's a world of great content to explore and magic to make.

Now it's time to put on your pointy hat, pull up your wizard's sleeves and let the dark crafting commence!

Dark craft disasters

One *last* thing before we get started is a friendly reminder that dark crafting – like any other crafting – doesn't always work out the way we want. The glue comes unstuck, the ink runs, the candle wax drips on the carpet, our love spell brings us that perfect person – who's moving to Uzbekistan. Things go wrong, and that's okay. It's all part of the process.

Intention is the only thing you really need to worry about getting right. If your intention is good, the rest will fall into place. If you have some screw-ups along the way, the best thing to do is learn and laugh. Actually, the best thing to do is learn, laugh and post a pic of your dark craft disaster on Instagram using the hashtag #darkcraftdisasters.

In no time you'll be forging a career as a magical influencer, promoting enchanted sex toys and holidaying in Transylvania. It's a charmed life!

PROJECT 01

A MAGICAL BATH

Since the beginning of civilisation, a good soak has been doing us wonders. Bathing hasn't just been about keeping clean and scrubbing pores – it's also played an important role in medicine, religion and community. People have socialised in public bathhouses, taken herbal baths to cure illness and immersed themselves in water for spiritual purification. Baths have also played an important role in magic.

The African-American folk magic practice of Hoodoo has a strong tradition of magical baths. Hoodoo baths typically include reading Bible verses aloud and mixing herbs, roots or oils into the water. Baths are used to inspire love, bring wealth and grant protection. They're also used to break curses and clear negativity. Taking a magical bath is standard practice before doing any kind of Hoodoo work.

Bath magic is now widely practised by modern magic-makers. After all, it's the perfect way to cleanse your aura and T-zone at the same time!

CURSE TABLETS

Archaeologists have discovered around 1600 so-called curse tablets dating back to ancient Greek and Roman times. These tablets were often made with lead, inscribed with curses (hence the name) and hidden away in temples, graveyards and wells.

Revenge was a major motivating factor for creating curse tablets. For example, this one was written by someone who was seriously pissed about getting their bling stolen:

> *[S]o long as [someone], whether slave or free, keeps silent of knows anything about it, he may be accursed in [his] blood and eyes and every limb, of even have all [his] intestines quite eaten away, if [he] has stolen the ring or been privy to [the theft].*

And if you thought that was bad, here's a guy named Verio who did not appreciate losing his coat:

> *The human who stole Verio's cloak or his things, who deprived him of his property, may he be bereft of his mind and memory ... may the worms, cancer and maggots penetrate his hands, head, feet, as well as his limbs and marrows.*

Some curses were much shorter, but still managed to pack a punch:

> *Tacita, hereby accursed, is labelled old like putrid gore.*

And this one:

> *May your penis hurt when you make love.*

SCENTSATIONAL

Making steamy magic

For your first step down the dark-crafting path, we want you to treat yourself to a lovely, magical cleansing bath! This is a simple and easy recipe for bath salts that will only take a couple of minutes to prepare. It's a potent recipe to quickly rid yourself of any darkness or ill will that might have stuck to you while you were scrolling X or getting your driver's licence renewed.

WHAT YOU'LL NEED

+ One cup of Epsom salts
+ A tablespoon (not 'of' anything … just the spoon)
+ A cauldron or standard-sized bowl
+ A teaspoon of activated charcoal
+ A tablespoon of rosemary
+ A tablespoon of lemon grass
+ Two drops of frankincense oil
+ A selection of white candles (as many as you can reasonably afford and/or fit around your bathtub without causing a fire hazard)
+ Matches or a lighter
+ A bathtub
+ A towel (we could go on, but you know how to take a bath …)

TIMING

Day of the week
Saturday

Phase of the moon
Waning moon

Step one

Put the Epsom salts in your cauldron or a bowl. Mix through the activated charcoal, rosemary, lemon grass and frankincense oil with a spoon.

Step two

Run a warm bath and pour in the bath salts. Light the candles and set the mood. Maybe put on some lo-fi or one of those 'energetic frequency' tracks that sound like whale song mixed with faraway roadworks. Whatever's going to help you relax.

Step three

Stay in the bath as long as you like (you don't need to be shrivelled like ET before you get out).

Step four

When you're done, pull the plug and watch the water drain. As the bath empties, visualise all the yucky energetic stuff you've have been carrying around going down the plughole. No need to worry about it anymore – it's the sanitation department's problem now.

Step five

Dry off and live your life!

PROJECT 02

A Witch's Broom

Nobody knows exactly when or how the tradition of the witch's broom began. Some say it started with ancient pagan fertility dances, while others suggest it kicked off with the Germanic goddess Holda. Maybe it's only right that it's hard to get a handle on the slippery history of the witch's switch.

What we do know is that the first pictures and written records of witches with brooms come from Europe in the 14th and 15th centuries. The case of Dame Alice Kyteler in 1324 is a good example. She was the first person ever sentenced to death for witchcraft in Ireland. The investigator in her case wrote:

> *In rifleing the closet of the ladie, they found a pipe of ointment, wherewith she greased a staffe, upon which she ambled and galloped through thicke and thin.*

Um … okay.

In the 15th century, some guy named Jordanes de Bergamo recorded this fun fact:

> *The vulgar believe, and the witches confess, that on certain days or nights they anoint a staff and ride on it to the appointed place or anoint themselves under the arms and in other hairy places.*

If you're getting a kinky drug vibe, don't worry – it's not just you. It was believed that witches rubbed a special 'flying ointment' into the broom handle, which was absorbed through their private parts when they straddled their broom. They would then fly off to cavort, make mischief and attend orgies. Sounds like a fun night out!

The theory goes that the ointments were made from hallucinogenic plants that triggered the feeling of flying. Maybe late-medieval witches were just tripped out on heavy-duty psychedelics? We can only hope …

A SCENE OF SORCERY.

THE WITCH CRAZE

The period from the 15th century to the 18th century was not a good time to self-identify as a witch in Europe. This was when the witch craze was at its height. Accusations of witchcraft could all too easily lead to imprisonment, torture and death. It is estimated that somewhere between 30,000 and 60,000 people were executed for witchcraft between 1427 and 1782.

With the anti-witch brigade out in force, deciding what was what and which witch was real was a crazy-making exercise in itself. This is particularly true when it comes to the methods used to identify witches.

One common method was finding a 'witch's teat' on the body of the accused. A witch's teat was a raised skin blemish believed to be a third nipple, from which imps or demons would suckle blood in exchange for granting magical powers. Having a mole or a birthmark was risky if you were a suspected witch.

Having a pet was also problematic. It was believed that certain animals – cats in particular – would act as familiars, assisting witches in performing magic and carrying out evil deeds. Having a pet cat could be a sign you were in a pact with the Devil. And sure, we all know cats have magic powers, but even so this seems a stretch.

If you were unlucky (let's face it – *everyone* accused of witchcraft was unlucky), you might be subjected to an ordeal by water. The accused would be tied up and dunked into a body of water. If they floated, they were deemed to be a witch and would be condemned to death. If they sank, they were innocent – but also dead from drowning. Effed either way.

Then there was the Bible-weighing test. The accused witch was weighed on a set of scales to determine if they weighed more or less than a Bible. The theory was that because witches could fly, they must be quite lightweight – and so, obviously, they would weigh less than a Bible. You might think this would be a dream test, because pretty much everyone weighs more than a Bible. Sadly, some accused witches still failed to pass this test … because the test was rigged.

The witch craze. Zero out of five stars. Would NOT recommend.

By the time we reached the 17th century, the 'witches riding broomsticks' meme had really taken off. It has remained an enduring pop culture reference ever since.

But there's another straw to the witch's broom tradition that has nothing to do with cheap air travel or getting high. It's the use of brooms to dispel negativity. We see this practice in folk and shamanic traditions all over the world: brooms are used in rituals to clear a place of all malevolent spirits and negative energies.

This is how most dark crafters use brooms today. It makes sense, really – what better way to sweep out bad vibes than by using something specifically designed for cleaning?

Making sweeping magic

Your witch's broom will clear away any sinister forces that might have crept into your home while you were watching *Keeping Up With the Kardashians* (truly a gateway to cosmic horror).

There are two options with this dark craft. The first is to make a regular, stock-standard broom. The other is to make a besom, which is basically a mini-broom (ideal for those hard-to-reach places). Both work the same – it just depends on how much room you have. If your lair is already a little cramped, a besom is probably for the best.

The instructions are the same for both. A besom is just smaller.

WHAT YOU'LL NEED

+ A branch or stick for the handle
+ Sticks of birch, wheat, lavender, tea-tree and rosemary for the brush
+ A ball of twine
+ A pot of craft varnish
+ A small varnish brush
+ A sheet of fine-grit sandpaper
+ A glue gun
+ A pair of scissors
+ A 10ml bottle of Frankincense

TIMING

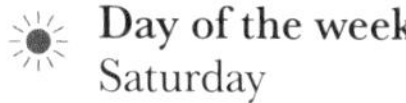

Day of the week
Saturday

Phase of the moon
Waning moon

Step one

Firstly, whack on some SPF 50+ and go for a walk in nature (or just down to your local park). Search until you find a branch that speaks to you. If you're making a broom, the branch should be approximately 120cm long. If you're making a besom, it should be approximately 30cm long.

Ideally, the branch has already fallen and is no longer attached to a tree. Don't go scaring the kiddies with hacksaws or the like. The idea is that the branch has been given to you by Mother Nature. And if she's not immediately forthcoming, that's just her way of telling you to stick at it.

Traditionally, witch's broom handles are made with hazelwood. However, any branch or stick that is sturdy and about the right length will work just fine.

Step two

Shape your broom handle so it's as user-friendly as possible. Don't worry, you don't have to get out your wood carving kit (unless you're an actual woodworker – in which case, good for you!). Just use your sandpaper to smooth off any sharp edges so you don't get splinters. Keep sanding until all the pointy bits are rounded off.

Step three

Apply a layer of craft varnish to the handle with your varnish brush. This will not only prevent cracking and keep your handle looking nice long-term, it will also seal your broom energetically. It's a win-win.

Step four

Now it's time to prepare the brush. This can be made with any kinds of twigs or sticks, but we recommend using birch, wheat, lavender, tea-tree and rosemary. If you can, pick (or buy) these fresh and hang them upside down in your home near a window to dry. The bonus is that this will instantly give your home that witchy cottagecore feel.

When everything has dried, tie the twigs and sticks to the handle with twine about a third of the way from the end of the handle. Wrap the twine around several times until the brush is secure. If you're having trouble securing your brush, there's no shame in applying some hot glue.

If you're making a besom, it may be necessary to trim down the brush so it's in proportion to the handle.

Step five

Anoint the broom by lightly rubbing the handle with frankincense oil. Once it's dried, you're good to go.

Step six

Now it's time to clean up! Grab you broom or besom and gently sweep along beside you. You only need to apply a light touch. Remember, a witch's broom isn't for sweeping up actual dirt (if you want to do that, just use a regular broom – or a vacuum cleaner). Move from the back to the front of your home. Once you reach the front door, open up and do a big sweep, expelling any nasties you've picked up along the way!

Repeat this once a month, ideally when the moon is waning (or whenever you feel like it).

• + •

BURNABLES

Another common tool for clearing is burnables – basically, stuff you burn.

The most well-known burnable for spiritual clearing is sage. The burning of sage is a long-standing Native American tradition. The sage smoke is wafted around people, places or objects to clear away negative energies. This is called smudging. The other top-ranking burnable is palo santo wood. This has been used by South American indigenous communities for centuries in a similar way.

As the use of sage and palo santo has grown popular, some have raised concerns. One objection is that the burning of sage and palo santo are indigenous traditions that have been culturally appropriated. The other problem is sustainability. The demand for sage and palo santo has led to overharvesting. This is bad for indigenous communities and bad for the environment. So if you're going to use sage or palo santo, do your best to ensure that what you use has been sustainably sourced.

If you'd rather avoid these issues altogether, a great alternative is dried rosemary. It's readily available and free of any ethical baggage. Just burn and waft!

PROJECT 03

A WAND

Magic wands have been pointing the way since ancient times. Here are just a few examples:

Thoth was the ancient Egyptian god of wisdom, writing and magic. He was often shown carrying a wand or a sceptre as a symbol of his power.

Chinese Taoist legend tells of sages using wands in magical battles to defeat enemies (which sounds incredibly kick-arse!).

Celtic mythology describes the magician Math using a wand to turn his nephew Gwydion into a deer, a pig and a wolf as punishment for bad behaviour (discipline was a bit unusual back then).

The ancient Greek messenger god Hermes was depicted carrying a wand, as was the ancient Greek goddess of witchcraft, Hekate, as was the ancient Greek god of medicine, Asclepius, as was the ancient Greek sorceress Circe … you get the gist.

Medieval and Renaissance spellbooks (also known as grimoires) describe the use of wands to create magical seals designed to harness supernatural forces. (Just to be clear, magical seals are symbolic drawings, not adorable aquatic mammals with mystical powers … unfortunately.)

One early example is a 13th-century grimoire called *The Oathbound book of Honorius*, which instructs magicians to hold a stick of laurel or hazel in their right hand when summoning demons to do their bidding. Summoning demons seems to have been the go-to form of occult outsourcing back in the day.

SUMMONING DEMONS

The Lesser Key of Solomon the King is one of the most infamous grimoires of all time. We don't know who wrote it, but evidence suggests it was compiled in the late 16th and early 17th centuries. *The Lesser Key* provides a how-to guide for summoning demons. It lists the names of 72 demons, along with their titles, appearances and job descriptions. Here are four to give you a taste:

DEMON 1

King Bael

Bael likes to mix things up – sometimes he looks like a cat, sometimes a toad, sometimes a man, sometimes all three at once! He has the power to make people wise, strong and invisible.

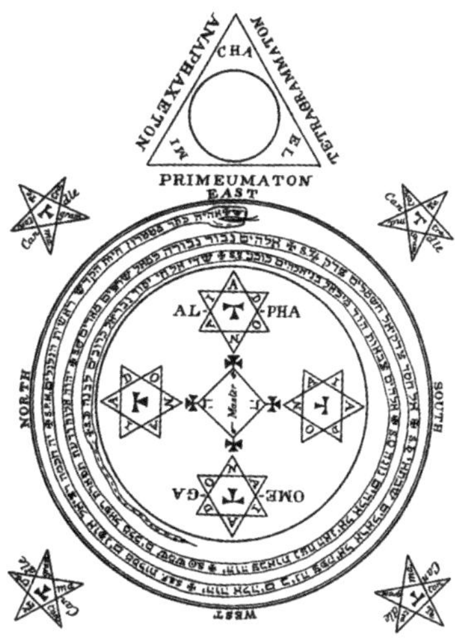

DEMON 7

Marquis Amon

Amon appears as a wolf with a serpent's tail. He can provide information about the past and the future, find lost objects and settle feuds. He also vomits fire, which probably means he has difficulty making friends.

DEMON 36

Prince Stolas

Stolas looks like an owl but with longer legs. He teaches astronomy and herbal medicine. He can also transform appearances (which is interesting, given he presumably chose to stick with the long-legged owl look).

DEMON 67

Duke Amduscias

Amduscias appears as a human/unicorn combo with wings (a bold look!). His arrival is accompanied by the sound of trumpets, and trees shake at the sound of his voice (#totaldiva). He specialises in granting musical talents.

If we're to believe the 2018 film *Hereditary*, summoning demons can cause such side-effects as insomnia, nightmares, insanity, broken noses, beheading, floating corpses and bursting into flames. So, if you want to learn the piano or astronomy or find your keys, it might be best to try other options first.

Other famous grimoires, such as *The Hepatmeron*, *The Picatrix* and *The Book of Abramelin*, also include the use of wands. These magical handbooks laid the foundation for our modern understanding of the wand as a tool for directing magical intention.

Making wand-erful magic

As a dark crafter, having a wand in your toolkit comes in super-handy when you're activating a spell. A wand is easy to use, powerful and looks cool!

WHAT YOU'LL NEED

+ A branch or stick for the wand
+ A glue gun
+ A pot of craft varnish
+ A small varnish brush
+ A sheet of fine-grit sandpaper
+ A ball of twine
+ A 10ml bottle of frankincense oil
+ Stones, crystals, charms, bells, dried flowers (basically, anything you want to decorate your wand with)

TIMING

Day of the week
Saturday

Phase of the moon
Waning moon

Steps one to three

These are essentially the same as the first three steps for making a witch's broom. Find an appropriate branch or stick, sand it down and apply a coat of craft varnish.

There are numerous recommendations for the types of wood that should be used when making a wand – hazel, laurel, elder, ash, birch, elm, holly, oak … the list goes on. As with the witch's broom handle, we suggest not getting too hung up on this. If you find a branch or stick that resonates with you, go with that. The main thing is that the wood you use should be durable.

As with many things in life, it's not the size that matters, it's how you use it. But a general rule is that a wand should be about as long as the distance between the tip of your middle finger and your elbow on the inside of your arm. But longer or shorter is fine. The important thing is that it's comfortable to hold in one hand and point.

Step four

Once you've completed steps one through three, it's time to decorate your wand!

If you prefer, you can skip this step. It's perfectly fine to work with a plain wand. But if a blinged-out wand is more your style, go to town!

Glue on any crystals or dried flowers that take your fancy. Use twine to tie on any small bells or charms. There's no 'correct' method for doing this. Your wand should be bedazzled in a way that feels right for you.

Sage

STONES AND CRYSTALS

Cultures the world over have believed in the mystical properties of stones and crystals. These shiny rocks have been a magical staple for millennia. They've been used in everything from amulets to alchemy to divination.

There's no shortage of books and online resources that explain the energies of stones and crystals. You're smart – you can google 'what does this crystal do?'.

But just to make your life easier, here's our top ten to get you started.

I. Amethyst for calming and intuition.
II. Black tourmaline for protection and grounding.
III. Clear quartz for energy and focus.
IV. Citrine for prosperity and abundance.
V. Hematite for absorbing negative energy.
VI. Lapis lazuli for wisdom and communication.
VII. Rose quartz for love and compassion.
VIII. Selenite for purification and clarity.
IX. Tiger's eye for strength and confidence.
X. Moonstone for emotional balance.

Step five

When you've finished decorating, it's time to get to know your wand.

Sit with your wand, hold it, feel its shape and contours. Listen to any messages it might be sending you (for example, 'I want to protect you', 'I want to empower you' or 'Damn, girl, you stuck more jewels on me than Rihanna at the 2018 Met Gala').

Don't worry if nothing much happens at first. Over time, you'll get a sense of what your wand is all about. The main thing is to establish a connection.

Step six

Anoint your wand by lightly rubbing it with frankincense oil. As you anoint, repeat this enchantment:

> *This wand is an extension of my spirit. Through the element of air, may it harness the strength and force of the wind as I conduct it at my will. Empower this wand with my magic. So mote it be!*

Now your wand is good to go. You can use it to imbue any magical item or spell with energy and intention – just point and focus.

If this doesn't make sense yet, don't stress. We'll provide examples later in the book of when and how to use your wand. In the meantime, just enjoy your fabulous magical pointing stick!

• + •

CANDLES

Another simple and easy way to activate a spell is to use a candle – just light up and let it burn. Job done! We'll give examples of exactly when and how to do this later in the book.

It's important to remember that, just like stones and crystals, different coloured candles possess different energies. It's essential to pair the right candle with the right spell. Here's a quick reference guide.

CANDLE COLOUR	ASSOCIATED ENERGIES
Red	Energy, strength, passion, courage, lust, love, vibrancy, element of fire
Orange	Business goals, property deals, ambition, career goals, justice, general success
Gold	Wealth, safety, happiness
Yellow	Intelligence, learning, memory, imagination, the element of air
Pink	Romantic love, healing, peace, affection, caring, nurturing
Green	Abundance, fertility, growth, personal goals, the element of earth
Blue	Good fortune, wisdom, inspiration, calm, creativity, the element of water
Purple	Psychic ability, spiritual power, self-assurance
Black	Protection, repelling negativity
White	Spirituality, higher-self, purity, the Goddess

We'll learn more about candle magic later …

PROJECT 04

A WITCH JAR

As far as dark craft projects go, it doesn't get much easier than a witch jar. It's literally just putting stuff in a jar. That's it.

Witch jars (or witch bottles) date back centuries. The first recorded description of a witch jar was written by the 17th-century clergyman Joseph Glanvill in his book *Saducismus Triumphatus.*

17TH-CENTURY UNSOLVED MYSTERIES

Joseph Glanvill wrote *Saducismus Triumphatus* to challenge society's growing scepticism about witches and witchcraft.

Saducismus Triumphatus.
Part the Second
W. Faithorne fec

People were beginning to wonder: 'Maybe the old woman next door with a mole on her cheek and a pet cat has nothing to do with my crops failing? Maybe I just suck at farming?'

This kind of scepticism ground Glanvill's gears, so he decided to document several real-life examples of ghostly and supernatural phenomena, including the infamous case of the Drummer of Tedworth.

The story went that John Mompesson, a magistrate from the English town of Tedworth, brought a legal action against a vagrant drummer named William Drury. Drury's drum was confiscated and given over to the magistrate. That was when things got weird.

Night after night, Mompesson's house was plagued by inexplicable drumming and thumping sounds. There were mysterious lights, unpleasant smells and flying objects. Glanvill visited the house and heard a 'strange scratching' coming from inside the children's bedroom. (Sweet dreams, kids!) This went on for years, until William Drury was found guilty of stealing a pig and shipped off to America. After that, the *Poltergeist*-style drama finally died down.

Although Glanvill failed to stem the tide of witchcraft scepticism (the witch craze was pretty much done and dusted by the mid-18th century), he succeeded in becoming history's first recorded paranormal investigator.

We're just wondering when the *Conjuring* spinoff franchise is going to come out …

At first, witch jars were mostly made as protection spells to ward off curses or evil spirits. In the days before burglar alarms, folk magic was the home-security system of choice. A common measure was to conceal witch jars in walls, mantlepieces, roofs and the like. The following objects were also hidden in homes to ward off evil spirits (including thieving relatives):

- ◊ Old shoes
- ◊ Horse skulls
- ◊ Dried-out cat corpses

That's right, people used to shove dead cats into their walls for magical protection … which gives a whole new meaning to 'pussy power'.

Срок годности: 24 месяца
Углеводы 98 г
+25°C
Масса нетто: 250 г
Дата изготовления:

Unsurprisingly, the original witch jars contained some hardcore ingredients (we're talking bodily fluids). Fortunately, things have got significantly more hygienic since then.

Nowadays, witch jars are used for everything from summoning success to healing illness to getting better options on Tinder. But as a nod to the old-school dark crafters, we're going to start you off with a protection spell. Don't worry – no horse skulls required.

ETHER C
R. CAMPHOR
SP. MENTH. P.
SP. LIMONIS
SYR. SCILL. C
EL. VAL. AM
COCULUS. IND
CARBO LIGNI
POT. BROMID
ANTHEM. GERM
P.R.SAR
F.E. TAR
F.E. CUBEB
F.E. ERGOT
F.E. SEN
SYR. S

CRAPPY INGREDIENTS

The *Greek Magical Papyri* is a collection of magical rituals and spells written on papyrus scrolls dating back to between the 2nd century BCE and the 5th century CE. These documents provide a fascinating insight into the religious beliefs and practices of the time. They also demonstrate how sorcerers back in the day were not afraid to get their hands dirty.

Among the hundreds of spells recorded in the papyri, a surprising number employ the use of animal dung. The collection recommends that if you want to make yourself invisible, you should 'take fat or an eye of a night owl and a ball of dung rolled by a beetle and oil of an unripe olive and grind them all together until smooth, and smear your whole body with it'. Sounds like a body scrub Gwyneth Paltrow might recommend.

There's a spell for getting a stubborn donkey to move, which involves smearing falcon dung and crocodile dung on the donkey's nose – eeeee-awwrgh!

There is also a spell to make a woman hate a man. Sure, some might say there's no special spell required. But hear us out – this one calls for dung, 'dead hair' and fresh flowers. Hey, it's the thought that counts.

Probably the most memorable dung-related spell is this oh-so-manly formula for love magic:

> *Crocodile dung, a little donkey placenta, and sisymbrium, 7 oipe of antelope dung, gall of a male goat, and first fruits of oil. You should eat them with flax stalks ... you should anoint your phallus with it, and you should lie with the woman ...*

'Nasty' doesn't even begin to cover it!

Making screw-top magic

This witch jar is designed to protect your home and family from malevolent forces, including that dodgy uncle who says he isn't racist, but …

WHAT YOU'LL NEED

+ A jar with a lid (a used jam jar is perfect)
+ A piece of paper
+ A pen (or a quill and inkpot if you're fancy)
+ A couple of peppercorns (or a sprinkling from your pepper shaker)
+ A handful of rose petals
+ A dash of salt
+ A sprig of rosemary
+ A teaspoon of chilli flakes
+ Two or three small nails (metal rather than toe)
+ One strand of your own hair (an eyelash will suffice)
+ A small black candle OR your wand

TIMING

Day of the week
Saturday

Phase of the moon
Waning moon

Step one

Grab your pen and paper. Write down the following: *Protect my home and family from all maleficent and unwanted energies.* (Throwing in words like 'maleficent' always amps up the magical intensity.) Fold up the piece of paper.

Step two

Put everything in the jar (except for the candle/your wand) and close the lid. Don't worry if it looks like a hot mess.

Step three

Now it's time to activate your witch jar.

You have two options for this:

I. Light a small black candle and sit the witch jar next to it. Let the candle burn down.

II. Take your wand and rotate the pointy end around the witch jar seven times in an anticlockwise direction (imagine your wand is a wooden spoon and you're stirring a pot of soup). As you move the wand, visualise an invisible bubble of protection surrounding your home.

Repeat this step every six months or so to keep your jar juiced up and ready for action.

Step four

Once it's activated, put the witch jar near the entrance of your home but keep it indoors. Nobody except you should ever touch your witch jar, so it's also a good idea to keep it hidden. (Pro tip: hide it in an out-of-commission sneaker. Nobody's ever touching that.)

Using the same four steps, you can make all kinds of witch jars. For example, here's the perfect get-witch-quick scheme …

• + •

A Witch Jar for Money

For this jar we suggest using basil, cloves and cinnamon. Add as much or as little as you like. We also recommend putting in actual money, in the currency you'd like to receive (smaller denominations are fine; there's no need to make it rain).

Write on a piece of paper how much money you'd like to receive. Try to keep it realistic. We're not talking Jeff Bezos penis rocket money here.

Once all the ingredients are in the jar, you can use a green candle or your wand to activate it. If you're using a wand, visualise your wallet filling up with cash.

Hide the jar somewhere you associate with money, such as your home office or where you keep your imitation Snoop Dogg gold chains.

PROJECT 05

A DEVIL'S TRAP

A devil's trap or demon's trap is a magical object designed to ensnare and disable evil spirits.

The earliest known examples are from ancient Babylon. Archaeologists have discovered numerous Babylonian 'incantation bowls' dating from the 6th to the 8th centuries BCE. Most of these bowls are inscribed with spells written in Aramaic. The writing is typically laid out in a spiral pattern, circling from the bowl's rim to the centre.

In some cases, bowls are also illustrated with pictures of tied-up demons, just to really drive home the whole 'Beelzebub in bondage' idea.

Incantation bowls were usually positioned face-down in the corners of rooms or near doorways to stop negative entities sneaking in through the cracks. Two bowls were sometimes glued together to make a sort of devil's trap ball – double strength!

Some bowls specifically named the demons they were targeting. A demon named on several incantation bowls is Pazuzu, whom you might remember as the demon from *The Exorcist*. Given the havoc Pazuzu wreaked on the little girl's complexion in that movie, it's not surprising they wanted to keep him at bay.

Other bowls were used as a form of magical weaponry. They were designed to capture demons so they could be unleashed on enemies – just like Pokémon.

LİLİTH

Lilith was a demon who often got name-dropped on incantation bowls. Here's an inscription from a bowl found in modern-day Iran:

The evil Lilith,
who causes the hearts of men to go astray
and appears in the dream of the night
and in the vision of the day,
Who burns and casts down with nightmare,
attacks and kills children,
boys and girls.
She is conquered and sealed
away from the house...

Lilith was a demon from Jewish folklore, although her name and characteristics are thought to have originated in a type of Mesopotamian demon called lilû.

According to Jewish legend, before there was Adam and Eve, there was Adam and Lilith. (Adam and Steve came later.) Unlike Eve, who was created from Adam's rib, Lilith was made from the same dust God had used to make Adam. Because Lilith didn't want to be a 'good wife' and obey Adam, she decided to leave the Garden of Eden. After a strong disagreement with three angels sent to bring her back, she was officially cast out. That was when she began her career as a full-time demon.

We might shout, 'You go, girl!' – only it seems that Lilith's main area of focus was murdering small children and seducing men (whom she would also murder). This didn't win her many fans. She was widely regarded with terror and contempt.

Her bad reputation remained intact until the 1960s and 70s, when women's rights activists reclaimed Lilith as a feminist icon. They celebrated her as a strong, bold and independent woman who was literally demonised for refusing to obey her husband. She wasn't a child-murdering villain – she was the original lady boss!

Since then, Lilith has become a popular symbol of female empowerment. Sarah McLachlan famously named her late-1990s feminist musical festival Lilith Fair. Magical practitioners have also embraced Lilith as a misunderstood and maligned goddess who embodies rebellion and sexual freedom.

From despised demon to beloved icon – talk about a glow-up!

Making demon-deterrent magic

If you want to make your own devil's trap, don't stress – you don't need to learn Aramaic or take pottery classes (although pottery classes are fantastic – very soothing).

We have a low-budget, low-skill, low-effort devil's trap recipe from American folklore that will enhance your home's magical security and give your place that *Blair Witch Project* vibe you've been longing for.

This type of devil's trap isn't designed to capture demons, so you don't have to worry about disposing of trapped entities in the recycling every two weeks. This trap works more as a 'Beware of the Dog' sign, scaring off any malevolent forces before they even reach the front door.

WHAT YOU'LL NEED

- Lots of sticks
- A ball of twine (black, red or natural colour)
- A pair of scissors
- A glue gun

TIMING

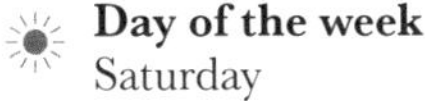

Day of the week
Saturday

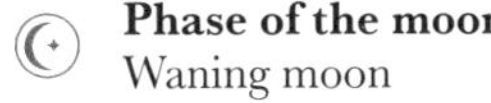

Phase of the moon
Waning moon

Step one

Collect a bunch of wooden sticks between 10cm and 30cm long. If you're feeling enthusiastic, you might like to track down sticks from a holly or hazel tree, which are traditionally associated with protection magic. But if that sounds like too much work, any old sticks will do.

The three longest sticks should be roughly the same size. They will be the base of your devil's trap.

Step two

Use the three longest sticks to build a tripod. Make sure the legs of the tripod aren't too close together at the base, as that will make the structure unstable. You want it to look more like a pyramid than a witch's hat. Tie the top of the tripod together with twine. Make the knot as secure as possible by looping the twine around several times.

Step three

Take a smaller stick and tie it onto two legs of the tripod like a rung on a ladder. If you have trouble tying the stick on with twine, use your glue gun. Don't worry about being symmetrical or neat. Be as wonky and messed up as you like. In fact, if the finished product doesn't look like it was constructed under the influence of mind-altering substances, pull it apart and start again. This devilish device of yours is supposed to look effed-up. Keep adding sticks at various angles. It's not necessary to cover the entire tripod with sticks. Just a few here and there until the structure is reasonably stable.

Step four

Once you've finished, attach a length of twine to the top and hang it near your front door or a window. If there's nowhere appropriate to hang it, you can always just sit it on a table. That's it! There's no need to activate your devil's trap – its appearance alone should be enough to frighten away any supernatural bad guys (or Jehovah's Witnesses).

If you decide to invite Satan over for a boozy brunch, we suggest hiding your devil's trap in the pantry beforehand – it's the polite thing to do.

• + •

THE DEVIL'S WEDDING

In the old town of Tallinn, Estonia, stands a 15th-century building with a strange story.

The legend begins with a hotel owner on the verge of a nervous breakdown. No clients, no money, no hope. All seemed lost when, one winter's night, there was a booming knock on the door. A tall man in a dark cloak stood on the doorstep, asking to hire the room on the top floor. He guaranteed the hotel owner an enormous sum of money if he promised that nobody would look inside the room while he was using it. The hotel owner happily agreed.

The tall man headed upstairs, and shortly afterwards a procession of extravagantly dressed guests arrived. They piled into the room, which started to rumble with laughter and music. The hotel owner was overcome with curiosity and decided to peek through the keyhole. Nothing could have prepared him for what he saw. It was the Devil's wedding.

Nobody knows exactly what the hotel owner saw or what happened next. Some say he died of fright a few days later. Others claim that after the guests had departed, the hotelier went into the empty room to find a bag of gold sitting on the floor. As soon as he touched the bag, it transformed into a pile of horse dung.

If you go to 16 Rataskaevu Street in Tallinn, you can still see the windows of the room where the Devil's wedding took place. They have been boarded up and painted over to stop any intruders climbing in. You can't visit the room, but you can visit the restaurant downstairs and enjoy a delightful three-course meal (vegan options available).

Just watch out for any tall men in dark cloaks …

PROJECT 06

PENDULUM AND BOARD

The 4th-century Roman historian Ammianus Marcellinus gives one of the earliest written accounts of pendulum divination. He describes a couple of guys predicting the name of the next emperor by hanging a ring from a piece of string over a dish engraved with the 24 letters of the Roman alphabet. After a priest wearing 'linen sandals' (interesting fashion choice) said some prayers, the ring-pendulum was set in motion over the dish, swinging back and forth. The ring pointed to the letters T-H-E-O. Turns out, the next emperor was Theodosius I – linen sandals guy was spot on!

The use of ring-pendulums for divination is called dactylomancy and was popular in medieval Europe. As in Roman times, pendulums were suspended over surfaces engraved with letters, numbers or signs of the Zodiac. But this wasn't the only option. Sometimes pendulums were held over body parts to detect illness, pregnancy or the gender of an unborn child. Pendulums were also used to detect hidden treasure, precious minerals or water underground (this form of divination is called dowsing and is also performed with forked sticks or metal rods). When there weren't any letters or symbols to point to, the movement of the pendulum itself was used to indicate 'yes' or 'no' – for example, swinging clockwise for yes and anticlockwise for no.

It became increasingly popular to use designed-for-purpose pendulums made from symmetrical, weighted objects hung from a chain, string or chord. The pendulum weight could be made of metal, wood, clay, stone or crystal. It was usually small and shaped like an onion, pear or cone. The pendulum could be placed in a pocket and easily whipped out for a quick spot of divination.

After going out of fashion for a few hundred years, pendulums had a revival in the first half of the 20th century. They were used in police work, archaeology, medicine and even the military. Having attracted all sorts over the years, these gadgets remain a popular divinatory tool today.

the
son of cups

DIVINATION

Almost everyone is familiar with astrology (astromancy), crystal balls (crystallomancy), palm reading (chiromancy) and tarot cards (taromancy). But there are plenty of other interesting forms of divination for the curious dark crafter to explore. For example …

Cromniomancy

When you think of fortune-telling, the word 'onion' probably isn't the first thing to come to mind. But there is a long tradition of onion-based divination that possibly dates to ancient Egypt (the ancient Egyptians were really into onions). In his 17th-century hit book The Anatomy of Melancholy, British writer Robert Burton describes the custom of women placing onions on an altar on Christmas eve to predict when they'll get married and how many husbands they will have (because just one is never enough).

Gastromancy

The ancient Greeks believed that they could hear the voices of the dead by listening to the sounds of a person's stomach. These stomach sounds were interpreted to predict the future. Gastromancy is even thought to have given voice to modern-day ventriloquism. So, on the list of things we can thank the ancient Greeks for, we can add that guy on stage with his hand stuck up a wooden doll.

Gyromancy

Remember as a kid when you'd spin round and round on the spot to make yourself dizzy? If that's something you still enjoy, you might want to consider a career as a gyromancer. This form of divination requires someone to walk in a circle marked with letters or symbols until dizziness makes them fall over. The meaning of the divination depends on what letter or symbol the person falls onto (use of padded clothing is advised).

Kephalonomancy

Have you ever wanted to track down a criminal but couldn't be bothered with all the police procedural work? No need to worry. Simply boil the head of a donkey and read aloud a list of suspects. The donkey's jaw will move when you read aloud the guilty person's name. Job done! (Actually, we don't recommend doing this, unless you're determined to make an ass of yourself.)

Molybdomancy

This form of divination involves interpreting the shapes formed by dripping molten metal into water. In Austria, Germany and Switzerland it is traditional to pour molten lead into water on 31 December to foretell the events of the coming year. In 2018, the sale of 'lead pouring kits' was banned by the European Union because exposure to lead can cause brain poisoning. Tin is often used as an alternative because it's less likely to kill you.

Rumpology

As you might have guessed from the name, rumpology entails examining the shape, size and qualities of the buttocks to predict a person's future. Jackie Stallone, the late mother of Sylvester Stallone, was a renowned rumpologist. Her cheeky claim was that the practice dated back to ancient Babylon; to date, no archaeological evidence of this has been uncovered, so we're not entirely sure where Jackie was getting her information. Anyway, Jackie would interpret photographs of buttocks emailed to her, as well as providing in-person consultations. She is said to have foretold the election of George W Bush to the US presidency by consulting the buttocks of her two Doberman pinschers.

Making divine magic

Having a pendulum and pendulum board is super-helpful whenever you're in need of some simple, direct cosmic guidance. It's also a straightforward method to master. There are no cards to memorise or astrological conjunctions to understand. It's just you, a pendulum and a board – the perfect starting point for any budding divinator.

WHAT YOU'LL NEED

+ A 4cm-by-4cm cube of air-dry clay
+ A 25cm length of twine (plain or any colour you like)
+ An embroidery needle
+ A 25cm-by-25cm wooden board
+ A sharpie (or paint and paintbrush, or woodburning implement, depending on your skill level)
+ A pot of acrylic craft paint (any colour you prefer)
+ A small paintbrush
+ A pot of craft varnish
+ A small varnish brush

TIMING

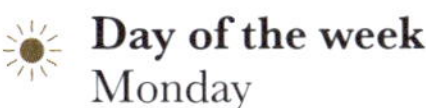

Day of the week
Monday

Phase of the moon
Waxing moon

Step one

Mould the clay into a cone 3cm to 4cm high. The base of the cone should be a circle around 2cm in diameter. Make the tip of the cone nice and pointy.

Step two

Stick the sharp end of the embroidery needle into the middle of the cone's base and push it about 2cm into the clay. Remove the needle and insert one end of the twine into the remaining cavity. Once you've inserted 2cm of twine, gently push the clay into the twine to secure it (making sure not to ruin the shape of your cone in the process).

Step three

Now that you've made your basic pendulum, leave it on a windowsill for a couple of days to dry. It's time to get started on your pendulum board.

Step four

With your sharpie (or paint and paintbrush, or woodburning implement), draw this template onto one side of the wooden board. Make sure your drawing covers as much of the board as possible. Feel free to add your own artistic flair as you go. If you want to draw witch's hats or stars or the cast of BTS around the edges of your board, go to town – we're not the design police.

Step five

When your drawing is complete, cover the board with a layer of craft varnish and leave to dry. Now, back to the pendulum …

Step six

Once the pendulum is dry, you can either leave it plain or you can add a coat of paint. There's no 'correct' paint colour for a pendulum, so just choose one that works for you. If you're artistically inclined, you can even paint small patterns or pictures onto the pendulum (provided you have a small enough brush, and it doesn't give you repetitive strain injury).

Step seven

Next up, leave your pendulum on your bedside table for three nights. We know this might sound a bit out there, but it will allow you to connect with your pendulum while you dream. Just go with us on this one.

Step eight

Now your pendulum and board are ready, it's time for some divination!

I. Place your board flat on a table in a position you can sit close to (as if the board is a placemat and you're about to have dinner).

II. Using your dominant hand, pick up your pendulum by the end of the twine. Rest your elbow on the corner of the table, near the bottom left-hand or right-hand corner of the board (depending on whether you're left-handed or right-handed).

III. Let your wrist flop so your arm resembles the head and neck of a stegosaurus. Your arm should feel stable, and the pendulum should be hanging over the middle of the board.

IV. Take a deep breath, close your eyes and think of a yes-or-no question you would like an answer to. When you're starting out, try to avoid major life questions like 'Should I get a divorce?' or 'Should I run away with my best friend on a road trip that results in homicide, a high-speed police chase and our untimely deaths?' … Keep it light.

V. Open your eyes but remain as still as possible. Eventually, the pendulum will start to swing. The direction the pendulum swings will indicate the answer – up and down for no, right and left for yes. If the answer is 'maybe', hold off on this question and ask it again another day. If the answer is 'rephrase', then do just that – think of another way to ask your question and try again.

VI. Once you've finished, use a burnable to clear away any undesirable energies that might have stuck to your board or pendulum while you were divining.

VII. As with anything, mastering the pendulum takes practice. If your answers seem a bit off at first, don't worry. It's just a matter of tuning into your intuition, which can be challenging at first if it's something you're not used to. If you keep working with your pendulum consistently, you'll begin to get clearer and more accurate answers. Never fear – you'll be finding stashes of hidden diamonds and predicting the winner of *The Great British Bake Off* in no time!

• + •

PROJECT 07

WITCH STONES

Lithomancy is any form of divination that uses stones. It would follow that it started in the Stone Age, but rock-solid evidence from way back then is thin on the ground. There is archaeological evidence of divination stones being used in Bronze Age Armenia (the Bronze Age was around 3000 to 5000 years ago). There is also some suggestion that lithomancy was used by the seer Helenus to predict the downfall of the ancient city of Troy, which is thought to have gone lights-out approximately 1200 BCE. Of course, when we get into the realm of thousands of years ago, it's hard to be super-confident about anything. Peeps weren't exactly wandering around with GoPros shooting travelogues.

There are several different approaches to lithomancy. One way is to hold gemstones and/or semiprecious stones up to candlelight and interpret the reflections they make. Another is to throw a collection of stones and read the patterns they form. A third option is to mark stones with symbols and draw them like tarot cards from a deck. This last option is the most popular among modern-day magic-makers, probably because it's the easiest to learn. (We don't know if you've ever tried memorising the hundreds of patterns stones fall into when they're tossed at random, but it's not a low-effort activity.)

Nowadays, many people work with runestones – divination stones marked with the runes of the ancient Germanic/Nordic alphabet known as Elder Futhark (try saying that seven times fast). Although it's true that runes have been associated with magic since the time of the Vikings, it looks like divination runestones only started to be used in the early 1980s, when the author Ralph Blum released *The Book of Runes: A Handbook for the Use of an Ancient Oracle* (the word 'ancient' was a bit of a stretch). This doesn't mean runestones aren't useful or important, though. Lots of important things came out of the 1980s: the personal computer, the internet, DNA fingerprinting, Madonna's *Like a Virgin*, leg warmers, perms and of course that other kind of weird sacred rock movement – Bon Jovi.

From the Bronze Age to the age of parachute pants, lithomancy remains alive and well in the world of witchcraft.

Mother Shipton.

From an Original Picture in the Possession of Ralph Ouseley Esq.

Making rockin' magic

Witch stones (also known as witch runes) work pretty much the same as runestones but with a different set of symbols. We don't know when or where witch stones were invented, so let's just say 'ancient Egypt' and move on with our lives.

Witch stones are effective and easy to use. They can help you foretell the future, understand the present and reflect on the past. Don't be deceived by the 'simple' symbols. Witch stones can be surprisingly meaningful once you get to grips with them.

WHAT YOU'LL NEED

+ 13 flat-sided pebbles of similar shape and size
+ A sharpie or permanent marker
+ A drawstring bag (you can make your own, but feel free to just buy one)
+ A piece of paper

TIMING

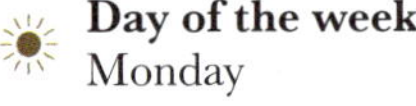

Day of the week
Monday

Phase of the moon
New moon

Step one

If you can, go down to a nearby beach or river or stream and collect 13 flat-sided pebbles of similar shape and size. Otherwise, you can just buy them online or at a garden supply shop.

Step two

Use the sharpie to draw the 13 symbols on the 13 stones (one symbol per stone). Here are the witch stone symbols with their associated names and meanings:

SYMBOL	NAME	MEANINGS
✷	**Sun**	Bravery, confidence, joy, new beginnings
☾	**Moon**	Dreams, intuition, mystery, secrets, uncertainty
🕊	**Birds**	Communication, messages, news, speech
◎	**Rings**	Alliances, bonds, connection, partnership, sharing
♥	**Romance**	Attraction, romantic love, sexual desire
♀	**Woman**	Gentleness, motherhood, nurturing, sisterhood, a woman
♂	**Man**	Action, brotherhood, dynamism, fatherhood, a man
✿	**Harvest**	Abundance, fruition, prosperity, wealth
◈	**Crossroads**	Conflict, irritation, obstacles, sacrifices, feeling stuck
∼	**Waves**	Change, emotion, spirituality
★	**Star**	Achievement, aspirations, hopes, a wish come true
☠	**Scythe**	Cutting off, danger, self-sabotage
👁	**Eye**	Attention, independence, the power of 'I'

Step three

Put the witch stones in the drawstring bag and keep them on your bedside table for three nights (see Step Seven in Project 6).

Step four

It's time to use your witch stones!

Start by asking a question and pulling one stone from the bag. Examine the stone's symbol and consider how it might answer your question. Read through the list of meanings and think about other meanings the symbols might have. Get creative. Remember, they're your witch stones. It's all about what the symbols mean for *you*.

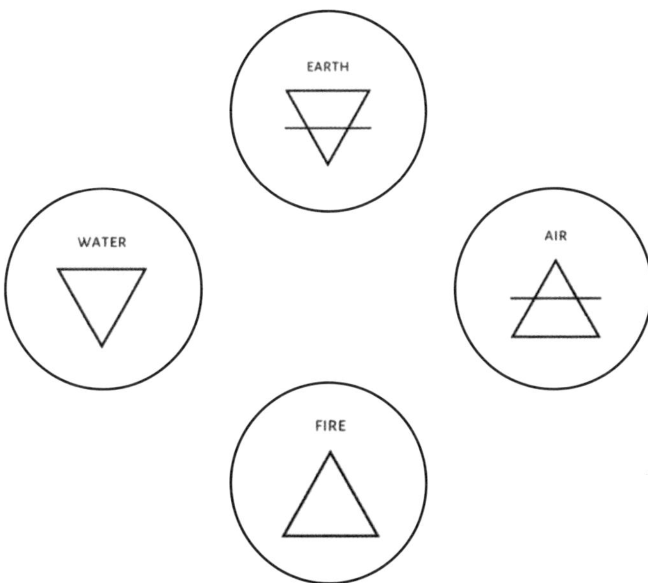

Once you've got to know your witch stones, you can start incorporating multiple stones into your readings. A good option is to use a 'divination spread', in which the layout of the stones tells a particular story or represents certain aspects of life.

The 'elements spread' is a divination spread that works with – you guessed it – the four elements! To begin with, take a piece of paper and draw the diagram pictured on the previous page:

Each circle represents the aspects of life associated with that element:

- **Earth:** Home and family
- **Air**: Intellect and imagination
- **Water**: Emotion and creativity
- **Fire**: Motivation and action

Pull four witch stones and place one in each of the circles. The witch stones will help you understand what's going on in each element of life. For instance:

- The sun stone in the water circle might indicate success in a new creative endeavour.
- The crossroads stone in the earth circle could mean conflict among family members.
- The eye stone in the fire circle may suggest the importance of standing up for yourself and forging your own path.
- The romance stone in the air circle might mean you're about to meet someone special with a high IQ.

It can be a good idea to keep a record of your readings and interpretations in a notebook. That way, you can look at past readings and reflect on the accuracy of your interpretations over time. This will help you better understand the messages your witch stones are giving you. You might discover that the eye stone in the fire circle has nothing to do with self-confidence, and is in fact a not-so-subtle hint to get your eyes tested.

Use your burnables to cleanse your witch stones after each reading, and have fun with fortune-telling!

MOTHER SHIPTON

On a dark and stormy night in 1488, a child named Ursula Sontheil was born in a cave in Yorkshire, England. She is said to have been born with a hunchback, a hooked nose and a natural talent for magic. Ursula ticked every box for 'stereotypical witch lady' from day one. Legend has it that she didn't even cry as a baby – she cackled. (That one is not super-believable, but okay.)

When Ursula was two, her mother gave her to foster parents and went to live in a nunnery. It was tough times for young Ursula, who was an outcast and regularly bullied for her appearance. In one account, teenage Ursula was walking past some local townsfolk who were hurling insults at her. She ignored them and kept walking. Later that day, one of the townsfolk realised that his neck ruff had turned into a toilet seat. Another discovered his hat had magically transformed into a chamber pot. Ursula knew how to clap back!

At the age of 24, Ursula married a local carpenter named Toby Shipton. Toby died two years later. Unsurprisingly, Ursula was accused of killing him with witchcraft. She decided to move back into the cave where she was born. To make money (those cave utility bills don't pay themselves), she worked as a herbalist and fortune teller. This is when she became known as Mother Shipton. She quickly became famous for the accuracy of her predictions, which she is said to have written down in the form of short poems.

The story goes that Mother Shipton accurately foretold her own death in 1561. She was gone, but her fame lived on. The first book of predictions supposedly written by her was published in 1641, followed by several other books. According to these, Mother Shipton correctly predicted Henry VIII's victory over France in 1513, the defeat of the Spanish Armada in 1588, the rule of Queen Elizabeth I and the Great Fire of London in 1666.

We're not entirely sure which of these predictions were actually written by her. The authors who published Mother Shipton's prophesies were often a tad creative with the truth. The most famous example of this is from a version of Mother Shipton's prophecies published in 1862, which included the prediction:

The world to an end shall come
In eighteen hundred and eighty-one

Spoiler alert: the world didn't end in 1881, and the guy who published the prediction later admitted to making it up. A lot of people have made up a lot of stuff about Mother Shipton over the past 500 years. It's impossible to say where legend ends and reality begins.

Whatever the truth is, Mother Shipton's legacy is still going strong. The cave where she lived is now a Yorkshire tourist destination, with a 4.2-star rating on Google. There is even a type of moth named after her. Mother Shipton for the win!

SPELL

PROJECT 08

A SELF-LOVE POPPET

The voodoo doll is perhaps the most recognisable symbol of malevolent magic out there. And who can honestly say they've never been tempted to use one? After all, it's only natural to long for the downfall of your mortal enemies … or your boss … or people who use the phrase 'Don't take this the wrong way, but …'

As with most pop culture references to the occult, the voodoo doll has been portrayed with about as much historical accuracy as *The Croods: A New Age.*

Let's start with the word 'voodoo' – that's wrong. The correct name is Vodou, which is a beautiful, complex religion that developed in

Haiti and blends elements of Roman Catholicism with traditional African beliefs and practices.

Then there's the doll. What most people know as a voodoo doll is actually a super-basic version of what in Vodou is called a *pwen* – a religious item used to summon and communicate with deities known as lwa. *Pwen* come in all shapes and sizes. While it's true that some *pwen* are crudely made dolls – referred to as poppets – it's not true that they're designed to harm people. In fact, *pwen* are mainly used to help and heal.

The *pwen* is just one example of the countless magical dolls, figurines and poppets that humans have been making for millennia. The ancient Greeks made *kolossoi* dolls that were used to bind spirits and deities. The ancient Egyptians fashioned figurines called *ushabti* that were placed in tombs to serve the dead during the afterlife. In Japan in the Edo period, young girls were given *hina* dolls to protect them from sickness and bad luck. In Guatemala, parents still give their children 'worry dolls' (*muñeca quitapena*) to take away their worries while they sleep.

Poppets are part of an age-old tradition that most likely has its roots in prehistoric times (like *The Croods: A New Age*). It goes without saying, no dark craft curriculum would be complete without learning how to make one!

SYMPATHETIC MAGIC

Sympathetic magic is the notion that you can cause real-life changes by using a symbolic representation of whatever it is you want to change. It's one of the earliest and most widespread magical ideas in the world. As described by the Scottish anthropologist Sir James George Frazer, there are two key forms of sympathetic magic:

I. Contact *(aka contagious magic)*: This is when you use a symbolic object that has had contact with, or is somehow connected to, the real deal. For instance, an object someone has touched or owns. Practitioners of malevolent magic might use a person's hair or fingernails to place a curse on them. (If you ever find yourself rummaging around in the garbage for someone's fingernails because you want to settle a score, please take a moment to reflect on your life choices.)

II. Similarity *(aka homeopathic magic)*: This is when you use a symbolic object that somehow resembles the real deal. Magical poppets are a perfect example as they are designed to look like human beings.

Sympathetic Magic
(*Laws of Sympathy*)

Homoepatic Magic
(*Laws of Similarity*)

Contagious Magic
(*Laws of Contact*)

Here's a super-fun diagram Sir James George Frazer made, just in case you were unclear.

Some examples of sympathetic magic include elements of both. For example, the Museum of Witchcraft and Magic in Cornwall, England, has on display a poppet made from red human hair that looks like a lady with a tight perm. It's a contact/similarity double-whammy.

Sympathetic magic has been a guiding magical principle throughout history. There is no end to the number of spells that incorporate elements of sympathetic magic, including a few of the spells in this book (remember the hair in the witch jar?). Once you start digging into more magic, you'll quickly realise how influential this idea has been. It's kind of like learning how to spot a fake Louis Vuitton bag – once you know how, you'll see them everywhere.

Making doll-ightful magic

When it comes to self-love magic, there really is no better option than a poppet. Not only are you harnessing the awesome and ancient power of sympathetic magic, you're also making a representation of your 'self' that you can take care of and shower with love. This is the stuff of emotional breakthroughs!

WHAT YOU'LL NEED

+ A 25cm-by-25cm square of pink felt
+ A 15cm-by-15cm square of plain cotton fabric
+ A pair of scissors
+ A pen
+ A tablespoon of dried rose petals
+ A tablespoon of dried jasmine
+ A tablespoon of dried passionflower
+ A spool of pink thread (preferably embroidery thread)
+ A needle
+ Two to three drops of rose oil or jasmine oil
+ A pink taper candle

TIMING

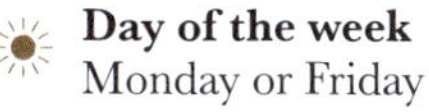

Day of the week
Monday or Friday

Phase of the moon
Full moon

Step one

Cut out a pair of body shapes with the pink felt. These cut-outs will form the basis of your poppet.

Step two

Take the piece of plain cotton fabric and write an affirmation on one side. Try to choose an affirmation that speaks to an area of self-love you might struggle with. If you have issues with your body, you could write: 'I am beautiful' or 'I am content in my body'. If you struggle to feel confident in relationships, you could write: 'I am worthy of love and respect' or 'I am more than enough'. Some more generic affirmations you could try are: 'I am joyful', 'I am loved', 'I am at peace' or 'I am Beyoncé'.

Once you've written down your affirmation, turn over to the blank side of the piece of cotton and write your name. (If you're a graffiti artist, feel free to use your tag.)

Step three

Take the rose petals, jasmine and passionflower and fold them into the fabric to form a small sachet.

Step four

With the needle and thread, sew up the poppet's arms, legs and torso, ideally using a blanket stitch. If you don't know how to do a blanket stitch, hop on YouTube and watch one of the many tutorials. Don't worry, you'll pick it up in no time.

Insert the sachet through the opening in the head area and then sew up the head.

Step five

If you like, leave your poppet as is. Otherwise, you can add some decorations. Sew on a face, attach buttons, bling it up in any way that feels good. Remember, your poppet is a representation of you, so feel free to decorate it in any way that feels true to you.

Step six

Anoint the poppet with rose oil or jasmine oil by applying a couple of drops to the chest area of the poppet (where its heart is).

Step seven

Get out your witch's broom or burnables and cleanse the space. Sit holding your poppet in your hands. Close your eyes and connect

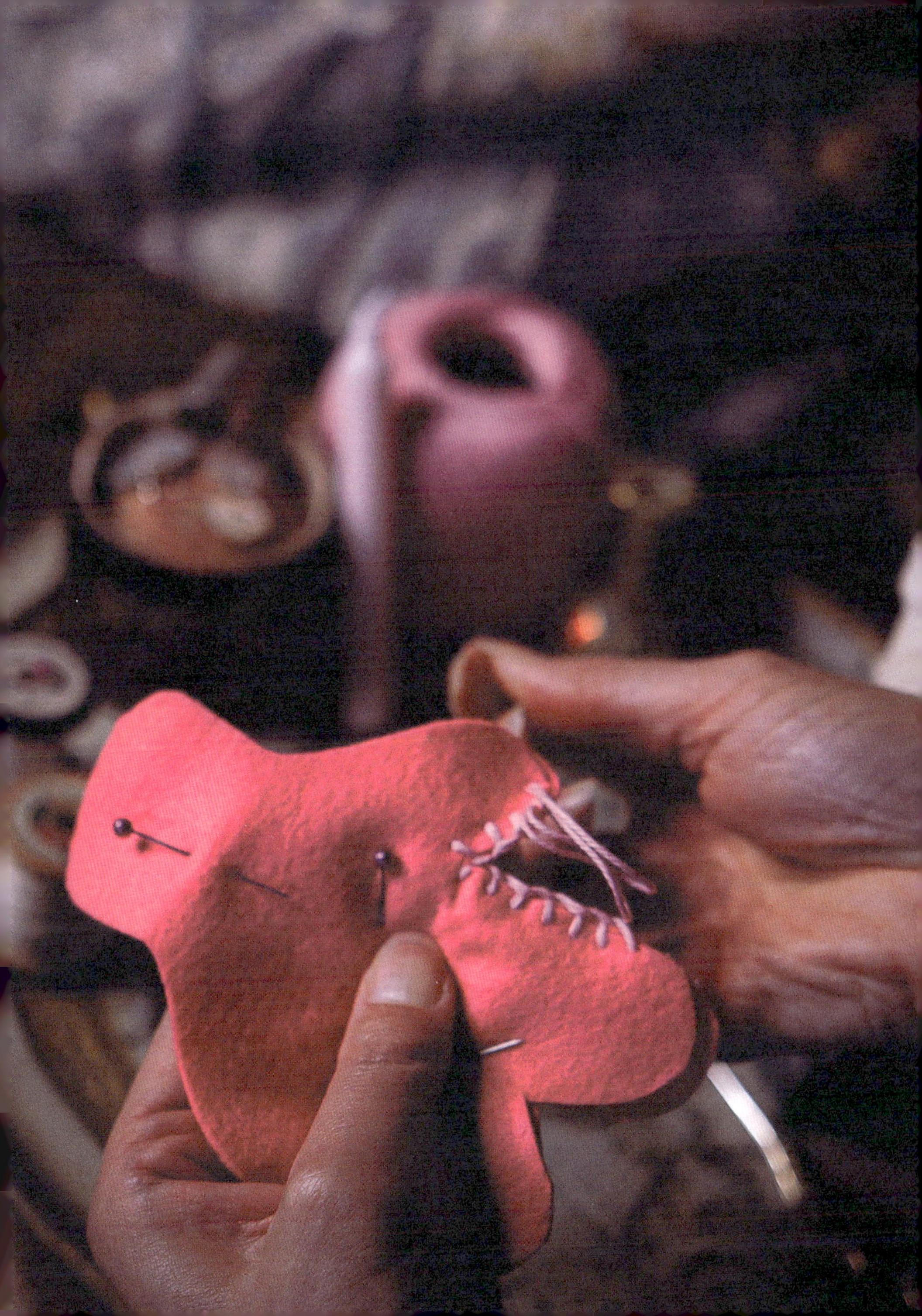

with your intention. Do your best to bring up a sense of self-acceptance and self-love. Spend five minutes doing this and then light a pink candle. Place your poppet next to the pink candle until it burns down.

Step eight

Tuck your poppet away somewhere safe – maybe in the same drawer where you keep your passport and vibrator. Leave it there and let it quietly do its magic. From time to time, feed your poppet by dabbing on some rose oil or jasmine oil. When you're feeling low on self-love, pull out your poppet and sit with it for a while. Let it remind you of what a wonderful human being you are.

In the wise words of Dr Seuss: 'Today you are You, that is truer than true. There is no one alive who is You-er than You.'

THE ISLAND OF THE DOLLS

South of Mexico City, tucked away in the canals of Xochimilco, is an unsettling little spot called La Isla de las Muñecas (The Island of the Dolls). As the name suggests, this island is a home for dolls – many, many dolls. They hang from the trees, they're nailed to fences, they lie on the ground. Everything the light touches is covered in dolls.

To be clear, we're not talking about fresh-out-of-the-box Barbies. Most of them are old, decaying dolls with matted hair, missing eyes and broken faces. Just delightful.

In the 1950s, a man named Don Julian Santana Barrera abandoned his wife and family to take up residence on the island. The story goes that Don Julian found the body of a drowned girl soon after his arrival. Later, he heard the voice of the dead girl shouting, 'I want my doll.' Don Julian returned to the place where he found her body and discovered a doll lying nearby. He hung it from a tree to make the dead girl happy (as you would).

After this, Don Julian became obsessed with finding dolls to decorate the island. He would retrieve them from the canals and recover them from people's trash (dead doll dumpster diving). Right up until his death in 2001, Don Julian was busy adding to his collection.

To this day, people bring dolls to the island to pay homage to the spirit of Don Julian and the drowned girl. The Island of the Dolls is a must-see attraction if you're visiting Mexico and enjoy the stuff of nightmares.

PROJECT 09

SELF-LOVE TEA

Legend has it that tea was first discovered by the Ancient Chinese emperor Shennong in the year 2737 BCE. The story goes that the Emperor was sitting under a tree one day, enjoying a cup of hot water. A leaf floated into his cup, turning the water a curious shade of brown. He must have been feeling particularly adventurous because he decided to take a sip. The emperor fell in love with the flavour and the beverage of tea was born.

Sadly, there's no historical evidence that this ever actually happened. What we do know is that tea was discovered in ancient China, where it was used for medicinal purposes. Tea became popular as a refreshing beverage in the Tang Dynasty (618–907 CE), and it was during this period that the first ever book on tea was published: *The Classic of Tea* by Lu Yu. The author was a monk known as 'the Sage of Tea' due to his extensive tea-related wisdom (everyone needs a hobby).

According to Lu Yu, tea was good for pretty much everything:

> *Tea tempers the spirits and harmonizes the mind, dispels lassitude and relieves fatigue, awakens thought and prevents drowsiness, lightens or refreshes the body, and clears the perceptive faculties.*

DYING TO STAY ALIVE

Around the time tea first became popular in China, immortality elixirs were also trending. While tea went on to become a worldwide phenomenon, immortality elixirs didn't really take off. This wasn't just because they were ineffective (as far as we know, nobody ever became immortal from taking one). The bigger issue was that immortality elixirs often proved to have unwanted side effects, including the most unwanted side effect of all – death.

There are a surprising number of Chinese emperors who are believed to have died in pursuit of eternal life. Immortality elixirs are thought to have killed a total of six emperors in the Tang Dynasty alone. Although future emperors exercised greater caution, it looks like elixir-related emperor fatalities were happening right up until the 18th century. Sometimes people just don't learn.

What was the problem with these elixirs? Nobody knows exactly. There is speculation that some included heavy metals such as mercury and lead, which aren't exactly things you want to consume if you enjoy being alive. Another possible ingredient was arsenic, which is a deadly poison. It goes without saying that the Taoist alchemists who whipped up these elixirs weren't always making the best choices.

An immortality elixir that kills you … isn't it ironic, don't you think?

Following its boom in China, tea soon spread in popularity throughout Asia and the Middle East. Europeans were late adopters and only started drinking tea in the 17th century, when Dutch traders imported it to Holland. Tea soon became popular with the English upper classes, and by the 19th century it was Britain's national drink. It was also around this time that tasseography came into fashion.

Tasseography (also known as tasseomancy) is a form of divination that interprets patterns in tea-leaves. Little is known about the origins of tasseography, but tea-leaf reading came into its own in Victorian-era England. It was popular to hire fortune tellers who would peer into emptied teacups and read the leftover tea-leaves. The tasseography craze hit a speed bump with the invention of the teabag in 1903 (an annoying by-product of teabags is that, unlike loose-leaf teas, they don't leave wet tea-leaves at the bottom of cups to be interpreted by fortune tellers). Tasseography endured despite this and remains a well-known form of divination in Great Britain and around the world.

Tea – it's a magical beverage!

Making a hot cup of magic

There's nothing quite like a cup of tea to warm the heart on a dark day. This is especially true when you add in a touch of magic. Here are two tea recipes to give you a special self-love boost on those days you need it most.

Rose tea

This is a soothing, supportive tea that harnesses the healing energy of water. It's perfect when you're feeling beaten down or having an attack of the 'not good enoughs'.

WHAT YOU'LL NEED

- 2 tsp of Earl Grey loose-leaf tea
- 1 tablespoon of rosewater
- 1 tablespoon of honey
- A cup of water
- Half a cup of milk (whatever kind you prefer)
- A handful of dried, edible rose petals
- A pinch of cinnamon
- A pinch of cardamom
- A kettle
- A teapot
- A strainer
- A teaspoon
- A saucepan
- A cup

TIMING

Day of the week
Monday

Phase of the moon
New moon

Step one

Boil the water and pour it into your teapot. Add the Earl Grey loose-leaf tea. Wait for five minutes for the tea to brew, then strain and fill half your cup with tea.

Step two

Warm the milk in your saucepan to your desired temperature, making sure not to let it burn (you're smart – you can work this out). Pour the hot milk into the cup until it's full.

Step three

Stir the rosewater and honey into the tea (add more or less honey to suit your taste).

Step four

Dress the top of your tea with a pinch of cinnamon and cardamom. Then sprinkle the rose petals on top with gay abandon.

Step five

Take the time to enjoy your tea in silence. Sit outside and watch the clouds go by. There's nothing to do but be.

TELLING THE BEES

According to ancient Egyptian mythology, bees were sacred creatures that were created from the tears of the sun god Ra falling to Earth (we're not exactly sure why he was crying, but it's good to know that ancient Egyptian deities were in touch with their emotions). It was believed that bees could cross the boundary into the afterlife and deliver messages from the dead. They were also a symbol of royalty. Bees were kind of a big deal.

As you'd expect, the ancient Egyptians were also into honey. In fact, they were the first people to make artificial beehives. Honey was called 'liquid gold' – it was used for food and medicine, as a ritual offering, and as a form of currency. It was even used in the embalming process, and pots of honey were placed in royal tombs. Fun fact: when the tomb of Tutankhamun was uncovered in 1922, they found a pot of honey which was apparently still good to eat after 3000 years! (Not sure who decided to taste the honey but thumbs-up for being an adventurous eater.)

Reverence for bees and honey is not uncommon. In ancient Greece, bees were a symbol of fertility and the goddess Artemis. According to the Kalahari San people of southern Africa, the bee played a vital role in the creation of humanity. In Hindu mythology, honey is considered a divine substance: there is even a bee goddess named Bhramari. Buddhists in Bangladesh and Thailand annually celebrate Madhu Purnima, the Honey Full Moon Festival. The list goes on …

In Europe, there is a custom called 'telling the bees', which became popular in England during the 19th century. This tradition involves informing the bees in your local beehive of any major life changes – birth, deaths, marriages, getting your roots touched up, et cetera. It's believed that if the bees are not looped into the latest family drama, they'll go into a passive-aggressive rage and stop producing honey. This tradition lives on: when Queen Elizabeth II passed away in 2022, the royal beekeeper is reported to have informed the bees at Buckingham Palace. The bees took the news as well as could be expected.

Cacao tea

This is a vibrant, uplifting tea that harnesses the invigorating energy of fire. It's perfect for when you need a healthy dose of 'You've got this, girlfriend!'

WHAT YOU'LL NEED

+ A heaped tsp of cacao powder
+ A tablespoon of honey
+ A cup of water
+ A quarter of a cup of milk (whatever kind you prefer)
+ A pinch of chilli powder
+ A pinch of salt
+ A kettle
+ A saucepan

TIMING

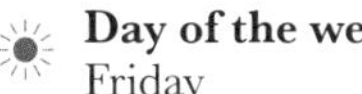

Day of the week
Friday

Phase of the moon
Full moon

Step one

Boil the water and pour it in your cup. Add the cacao powder, honey, chilli powder and salt, then stir.

Step two

Warm the milk in your saucepan and add to the tea.

Step three

Turn on your favourite tunes and enjoy your tea with a slice of something delicious. The world is your number-one fan!

• + •

FOOD OF THE GODS

The Mesoamericans were the first to discover chocolate. In fact, chocolate derives its name from the Aztec word *xocoatl*, which means 'bitter water'. The Aztecs called chocolate 'the food of the gods' and associated it with the feathered serpent god Quetzalcoatl. Unlike the sweet treat we know today, the Aztecs consumed chocolate as a cold, frothy drink that tasted quite bitter. Chocolate was renowned as an aphrodisiac: it's said that the Aztec ruler Montezuma II enjoyed 50 cups of chocolate a day. (He had two wives and countless mistresses, so we suppose he was just trying to keep up!)

When the Spanish conquistadors invaded in the 16th century, they decimated the Aztec civilisation and stole their chocolate. This was when chocolate took off in Europe and became famous as a dessert. Meanwhile, the Spanish colonial government did its best to stamp out the traditional reverence for chocolate in Latin America. Records show that a surprising number of alleged witches were accused of using chocolate in their witchcraft. In one account, a woman and her daughter landed themselves in prison because they were accused of mixing their pubic hair in a cup of chocolate and serving it to the local village priest!

Despite the Spanish Inquisition's best efforts, chocolate never lost its magical flavour. Films such as *Willy Wonka & the Chocolate Factory* and *Chocolat* remind us that nothing quite inspires our sense of wonder like a mouthful of delicious chocolate.

PROJECT 10

A CANDLE SPELL

We've already described how candles can be used for activating spells. But candles don't just play a supporting role. They can also take centre stage!

There are well-established candle magic traditions in European, African-American and Mexican folklore. While practices vary widely across cultures, candle magic often involves the use of coloured candles inscribed with words or images and anointed with oils.

An important aspect of candle magic is that it calls on all four elements, not just fire. Air is harnessed via the oxygen that feeds the flame, the solid candle represents the grounding of earth, and the melted wax invokes the fluid nature of water. Although candle magic might seem simple, it's remarkably holistic and powerful – like Beyoncé.

Making flaming magic

We can all agree that candlelight is romantic. It's right up there with rose bouquets, Paris at night and giant cheques for $17 million. And what better way could there be to put the spark back into your dating life than with a candle spell for love?

This love spell is designed to get the right person swiping right with minimal fuss. It is significantly less expensive than hiring a Netflix-series matchmaker, and MUCH less traumatic than appearing on *Married at First Sight*.

TAINTED LOVE

The ancient Athenian speechwriter Antiphon tells a dark story of love magic gone wrong.

Antiphon describes a woman (let's call her Joanne) who wanted to kill her husband (let's call him Neil). Neil liked to enjoy a beverage with his friend Philoneos, so Joanne convinced a concubine who had a crush on Philoneos to pour a 'love potion' into his and Neil's wine. Joanne told the concubine that the potion would reignite Philoneos' affection for her. This was somewhat misleading, as the love potion was actually poison. As Antiphon tells it:

> *[T]he concubine slipped the poison into the wine she was pouring out for them: and furthermore, thinking that she was doing something clever, she gave Philoneos an extra dose, supposing that the more she gave, the warmer would be his love for her.*

Philoneos died on the spot. Neil died a few weeks later. The concubine was tortured and murdered. Joanne's fate is lost to history.

This story shows how widely accepted love magic was in ancient Athens. It's also a reminder to check your potion ingredients for nuts, gluten and deadly toxins.

(C'est celui d'Azay-le-Rideau en Touraine).
fabriqu d'admirables
couleurs éclatantes.
dans les
gneurs, des
, des bour
châteaux
Ces châ
x de la R
qu'on bâtissait au
Depuis que les
igneurs ne

WHAT YOU'LL NEED

- Two pink taper candles of 20cm to 30cm in length, either plain or 'person-shaped' (we'll cover what that means in Step One)
- A dinner plate (although not your grandmother's fine china – things are gonna get messy)
- A small dish
- A knife
- Matches or a lighter
- Ten (or more) pins
- A metre of pink twine or thread
- Half a cup of rose petals
- Three drops of rose oil
- Three drops of jasmine oil
- Your wand (optional)

TIMING

Day of the week
Friday

Phase of the moon
Full

Step one

Get two pink candles. These can be plain taper candles, or you can buy two person-shaped candles. Typically, these are moulded in the shape of a naked standing figurine; they come in either a male or female form.

You'll need to mix and match the genders of the candles according to your sexual preferences. If you are bisexual, pansexual or otherwise don't care about the gender of your romantic partner, you might like to use a person-shaped candle for yourself and a plain taper candle for your significant other. If you are trans or gender-fluid, please don't hesitate to do a spot of carving to make your candles truer to reality. It's important you feel comfortable with the candles you're working with.

If you can't find or alter person-shaped candles so that they feel authentic for you, we recommend just sticking with plain taper candles. Emotional and spiritual comfort is key when it comes to dark crafting.

Step two

Choose the candle that represents you and scratch your name into it with a knife; just your first name is fine. Leave the other candle blank, or scratch in the name of someone you have your eye on. However, if you choose to do this, we must offer a warning …

A HEADS-UP

Magic can't force someone to fall in love with you. If the spark isn't there, or if you're wishing for something entirely outside the realms of possibility, it's not going to happen. Carving 'Ryan Gosling' or 'Eva Mendes' into a candle probably isn't gonna work. This magic can only encourage something that has genuine potential.

If you've really zoned in on one person, you might want to take a step back before you go harnessing any cosmic forces. That fabulous jacket you found online might look like a potato sack when you try it on at home. Be careful what you wish for.

Step three

Mix the rose oil and jasmine oil together in a small dish and use the combined oil to anoint the candles. Just dab the oil on your fingers and, starting at the base of each candle, spread it upward. Repeat this process until the candles are pretty much covered in oil.

Step four

Take a moment to sit with your candles. Close your eyes and visualise life with your prospective partner. Then pick up your pins and start inserting them into the candles.

THE POSITIVES OF PINS

In popular culture, using pins or needles in magic is usually a bit of a downer. The classic image is of a voodoo doll getting stabbed with rusty nails. Cut to some random person screaming, 'My arm! My leg! My brain! What's happening to me?'

As we've already discussed, the pop culture version of the voodoo doll is total fake news. While it's true that pointy things can be used for harmful magic, they can also be used for positive purposes. In this spell, the pins are used to 'drive in' the energy of what you're trying to achieve. Think of it as an injection of romantic vibes into each of the candles. As with everything in dark crafting, it's all about intention.

Insert the pins into any part of the candle that feels right for you. As you go, try to keep your mind on all the fabulous romance coming your way! Finish up when you feel complete (or when you run out of pins).

Step five

Stand both the candles in the middle of the dinner plate, as close together as possible. If you're using person-shaped candles, position them so they're facing one another. If the candles won't stand up on their own, feel free to use some Blu Tack to secure them to the plate. It won't ruin the magic, we promise.

Step six

Sprinkle the rose petals so they create a nice bed at the base of the candles. You don't have to be too extra – this isn't a Bollywood wedding.

Step seven

Take the length of pink twine or thread and wrap it around the candles. Start at the top and work your way down, binding the two candles together. Think of all the amazing adventures you'll have with your new romantic partner, both in and out of the bedroom. Once you've finished this process, tie the twine or thread off.

Step eight

Light the candles and position your hands above them in blessing gesture (palms down, fingers spread slightly apart), or get out your wand and point it towards the candles. Say this enchantment three times:

> *I call upon the energies of love. I summon the powers of love and attraction. Bring my lover to me. As I will it, so mote it be!*

Step nine

Let the candles burn down as close to the bottom as possible (preferably the bottom of the candle, not the posteriors of the figures themselves – but hey, you do you). If you have to pop out for a spa date or to help your bestie bury a body, don't stress. Just blow out the candles and relight them when you get back. It really takes the shine off finding that special someone if you burn your house down in the process. Always keep your dark crafting fire-safe.

Also, please don't expect your special someone to appear on the doorstep, ready for action, five minutes after you've finished this spell. Letting go of expectations is an important part of magical practice. In fact, putting pressure on magic can energetically block your intention. Just let it go and live your life. The surprise will be worth it.

• + •

More candle magic

Now that you have the basic steps, you can perform all kinds of candle magic. The good news is that most candle magic doesn't require too many ingredients. All you need for a stock-standard candle spell is:

- ◊ A candle
- ◊ A knife
- ◊ Anointing oil
- ◊ Matches or a lighter

You take a candle, make an inscription, anoint it with oil and light it up – job done.

Here's an easy-to-use candle magic reference table:

TYPE OF SPELL	COLOUR OF CANDLE	WHAT TO INSCRIBE	ANOINTING OIL
Happiness	Yellow	Write a positive word or scratch on a smiley face.	Lemon
Healing	Blue	Write the name or draw the part of you that you wish to have healed (e.g. lungs, nose, brain).	Chamomile
Money	Green	How much money you need.	Basil
Protection	Black	Carve a hand into the candle. (Hands are hard to draw in wax but just do your best.)	Rosemary

And don't forget, **ALWAYS KEEP YOUR CANDLE MAGIC FIRE-SAFE!**

• + •

PROJECT 11

SIGIL MAGIC MAKE-UP

Images and symbols have always been a big part of magic. There is evidence that even Neolithic people, who were living their best lives around 12,000 years ago, carved symbols into stone for supernatural reasons. Alchemical glyphs, Babylonian seals, Chinese pictograms, Egyptian hieroglyphs, runic talismans – images and symbols have been used throughout history to represent and harness otherworldly forces.

Renaissance grimoires were often illustrated with pictures called sigils. These pictures were designed to invoke spirits (usually angels or demons). It was believed that a spirit's sigil was directly connected with that spirit's energy. A magician could summon a spirit by using the spirit's sigil in a ritual. (Think Uber Eats, but you're using a ritual instead of a smartphone, and you are delivered an angelic or demonic spirit instead of dumplings.) Following are some examples of Renaissance-era sigils.

The sigil of the archangel Gabriel from *The Heptameron*:

The sigil of the demon Lerage from *The Lesser Key of Solomon*:

The sigil of Jupiter (Berthor) from *Arbatel De Magia Veterum*:

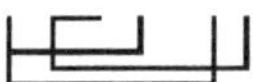

As you can tell, these sigils don't really look like anything. They were thought of more as signatures than as symbols – perfect for when a demon needs to sign off on their gym membership.

THE GREAT MAGICIAN WIFE SWAP

Dr John Dee was a 16th-century astrologer, astronomer, alchemist, mathematician, teacher, writer and political adviser to Queen Elizabeth I (total overachiever). He was also a magician who invented the 'Enochian magic' system with his friend Edward Kelley.

Enochian magic is based on communication with angels. Dee and Kelley spent countless hours writing down angelic messages; they even documented an entire Enochian language. They weren't messing around.

By all accounts, Dee was a firm believer in Enochian magic. As for Kelley, the jury's out. Before teaming up with Dee, Kelley had a reputation as a con artist and was a convicted counterfeiter. When they met, in 1583, Dee was on the lookout for a medium who could help him communicate with the spirit realm. Kelley claimed to be a gifted spirit medium, although there's no record of him practising mediumship beforehand. It's all a tad suspicious.

Anyway, Dee hired Kelley to help with his occult investigations and for a while they were the magical dream team. However, things went downhill in 1587, when an angel allegedly told Kelley that the duo should spend the night with each other's wives. According to Kelley, it was all part of God's grand plan to 'unify' the pair. Dee and his wife, Jane, were less than impressed. They only agreed to the swap because they didn't want to disappoint God. Nine months later, Jane Dee gave birth to a son … you do the maths.

The duo's angel communication sessions dried up after the wife swap. (Perhaps Dee was worried the angels would tell him to get a face tattoo or a nipple piercing.) Dee and Kelley parted ways in 1589. To nobody's surprise, Kelley spent the rest of his life in and out of prison. He is said to have died in a failed jailbreak in 1598. A sketchy end for a very sketchy guy.

The early 20th-century English occultist Austin Osman Spare had a fresh take on sigils. He believed they were tools for focusing magical intention. Spare would make his own sigils by writing a 'statement of desire' – for example, 'I want a salted caramel cheesecake' – and then using the letters in the statement to create the sigil. He would then charge the sigil through a variety of methods, including visualising it while he was orgasming! According to Spare, the main thing was to 'implant' the sigil in the magician's mind. Once the sigil had been 'absorbed', it would work its magic by harnessing the power of the unconscious.

Spare's ideas were taken up by the modern 'chaos magick' movement, which is based on rejecting dogma, forging your own path and boiling down magic to what really works. It's basically magical anarchism for the new age. Sigil magic is a big-time practice for chaos magicians, including the comic-book writer Grant Morrison. He credits sigil magic with helping his career and saving his comic book series *The Invisibles* from cancellation.

Morrison also describes a more sinister side to sigils. He believes logos like the McDonald's golden arches and Disney's Mickey Mouse ears are 'viral sigils' that infect the minds of consumers. So the next time you see the Nike swoosh or the Target target, it's worth considering whether you're being exposed to a form of corporate sorcery.

SIGIL SEX MAGIC SUCCESS

Grant Morrison's *The Invisibles* is a mind-bending kaleidoscope of sorcery, psychedelics, aliens, fetish clubs, quantum physics and conspiracy theories. It follows a ragtag team of magical terrorists fighting an oppressive regime led by the monstrous, interdimensional 'Archons of the Outer Church'. It's one hell of a read!

Published between 1994 and 2000, *The Invisibles* is now a cult classic. But in 1995 it was almost cancelled. Although the first issues were well received, readership soon dropped off (the subject matter being a bit 'out there' for some people). Eager to keep his comic alive, Morrison reached out to the fans and asked them to engage in some supportive sigil magic. He instructed them to make a sigil designed to rescue the comic and asked everyone to charge their sigil on the night of Thanksgiving by visualising the sigil as they masturbated. (Hopefully everyone had finished their Thanksgiving dinner first!)

While it's unclear how many people participated in this en masse magical masturbation event, it seems to have done the trick. *The Invisibles* was renewed and a total of 59 issues were released. In 2019 Rolling Stone magazine listed it as one of 'The 50 Best Non-Superhero Graphic Novels' of all time.

Sigil sex magic making it work!

TABU
TABU
TABU
$2.50
tax extra
Lipstick
TABU
ith concealed vial of the famous "forbidden" perfum

Making make-up magic

'Glamour' isn't just a term for describing Hollywood stars, fashion models and drag queens – although I think we can all agree that Sasha Velour's lip-sync at the end of season nine of *RuPaul's Drag Race* was the definition of glamour!

The word 'glamour' comes from the early 18th-century Scots word *glamer*, meaning 'magic spell' or 'enchantment'. A glamour was originally a kind of spell cast to create an illusion. Over time, this idea evolved into what we now call glamour magic.

Modern glamour magic is less about deceiving people and more about bringing good things into your life through the power of attraction and allure. Of course, it makes sense that one of the easiest ways to perform glamour magic is to put a spell on your make-up!

This dark craft uses sigil magic to give your make-up an enchanted edge. It will help attract pretty much anything you desire, but is particularly useful if you're on the lookout for that special someone. If you don't wear make-up, don't worry – it works just as well with a bottle of moisturiser or sunscreen. You'll be glowing with supernatural radiance in no time!

WHAT YOU'LL NEED

+ A pen
+ Paper
+ An item of make-up (pressed powder foundation is a good option, but you can use pretty much any foundation, lotion or moisturiser)
+ A pink taper candle
+ Matches or a lighter

TIMING

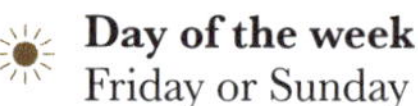

Day of the week
Friday or Sunday

Phase of the moon
Full moon

Step one

Write one of the following affirmations on a piece of paper:

- ◊ I am attractive
- ◊ I am beautiful
- ◊ I am desirable
- ◊ I am divine
- ◊ I am gorgeous
- ◊ I am radiant
- ◊ I am stunning
- ◊ I am whole

Step two

Go through and cross out any vowels or repeated letters in your affirmation. For example, the affirmation 'I am attractive' will look like this:

~~I~~ ~~A~~M ~~A~~~~T~~~~T~~R~~A~~C~~T~~~~I~~V~~E~~

Now write out the remaining letters. For 'I am attractive', these will be MRCV.

CHAPTER SEVEN

Step three

Use the remaining letters to form your sigil. Here's an example of a sigil made using the letters MRCV:

Step four

Once you've made your sigil, draw it into or onto your item of make-up. Pressed powder foundation is good because you can draw the sigil directly into the powder. (If you don't want to get ink in your foundation, use a sewing needle to draw the sigil.) If you can write small enough, you can scratch the sigil into your lipstick. If you're using a bottle of lotion or a jar of face cream, just draw the sigil onto the bottle, jar or packaging. Feel free to play around with options. The important thing is that the sigil is somehow imprinted on the item of make-up.

Step five

Activate the sigil by sitting your item of make-up next to a pink taper candle and lighting up. Once the pink taper candle has burnt down, you're good to go.

Alternatively, you could activate your sigil using the 'visualising at the point of orgasm' method. There are plenty of online resources to tell you how. You do you … literally.

Step six

Apply your sigil magic make-up and take yourself out on the town! Share your divine beauty for the world to enjoy! Own it, live it, love it!

• + •

II
The
Priestess

PROJECT 12

A CHARM BAG

There is likely no dark craft as ancient or as universal as the use of charms – magical objects that are either worn as jewellery or carried around, usually for protection or to bring good luck. It's something people have been doing everywhere forever.

Magical charms fall into two main categories: amulets and talismans. The difference can be kind of vague, like the difference between creative accounting and white-collar crime. To keep things simple, let's just say that amulets are objects that naturally possess magical qualities, while talismans are carved or inscribed to become magically powerful, sometimes with the help of a spell or ritual.

Charm bags are something of an amulet/talisman grey area. They are small bags filled with magically potent objects. They can be made for anything from attracting wealth to repelling enemies to improving action in the bedroom. Charm bags are often stuffed with amulets – such as stones or crystals – as well as with dried flowers and herbs. They can also hold talisman-type objects, like spells or sigils written on wood or parchment. They are usually worn as a pendant or kept in a pocket.

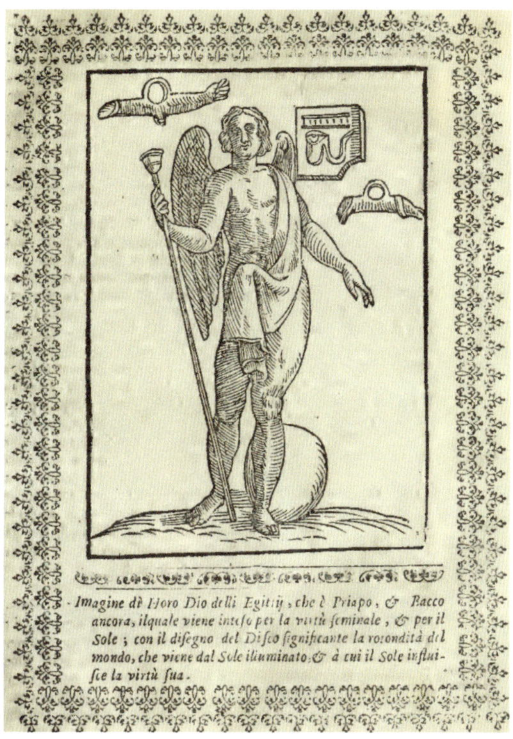

NOT-SO-CHARMING CHARMS

When asked to name a good luck charm, most people think of a horseshoe, a ladybird or a four-leaf clover. These are the stock-standard, norm-core lucky charms that decorate lottery scratch cards and casino slot machines. But there are plenty of others that are less well known, and a tad more bizarre.

Did you know that in some parts of the world the head of a vulture is believed to bring good luck in gambling? This is based on the belief that vultures can foretell the future. The logic goes that having a vulture's head nearby will bless gamblers with similar foresight: sort of an occult transferable skill.

Back when public executions were all the rage, a hangman's rope was a lucky charm for gamblers. In fact, these became so highly prized that hangmen would sometimes cut them up into smaller pieces following an execution and sell them off. (Classy!) Pre-used nooses were also believed to cure illness. Sick people were known to hang them around their necks to help along the recovery process. (Super-classy!)

In ancient Rome, carvings of penises with wings were the go-to good luck charm of the time. Known as the *fascinus* or *fascinum*, this represented the 'divine phallus' and acted as protection against bad luck or ill will. People would wear be-winged penises as jewellery and have statutes of them around the house – which we're sure you'll agree is quite a bold interior design choice, and a whole lot classier than a dick pic.

Then there are bezoars: small stones made from undigested or partially digested matter found in the gastrointestinal tracts of goats, sheep, deer and other animals. These delightful little objects were popular in the Middle Ages as protective amulets. (Apparently Queen Elizabeth I wore a bezoar set in a silver ring.) Bezoars were thought to cure illness and serve as an antidote to poison. When King Charles II was on his death bed, his doctors gave him powdered bezoar stone along with other groundbreaking medical interventions, including 'human skull extract' and a poultice of burgundy pitch and pigeon dung applied to his feet. To everyone's surprise, King Charles II still died. Unlucky.

Making charming magic

We all need a confidence boost now and again. Sometimes listening to a Tony Robbins podcast or spending five minutes in a power pose just isn't enough to brush away the sticky webs of self-doubt. This is where a confidence charm bag can come in handy, providing that extra magical dose of self-belief!

WHAT YOU'LL NEED

+ A 13cm-by-13cm square of orange fabric (cotton or linen)
+ A tablespoon of butterfly pea flower (it's a herb)
+ A tablespoon of thuja (you guessed it – a herb)
+ A tablespoon of horsetail (also a herb – not from an actual horse)
+ A tuft of cornsilk
+ A tumbled sunstone (or you can use red jasper or carnelian – whichever works for you)
+ A small piece of paper
+ A pen (or quill and ink)
+ A metre of leather (or faux leather) cord
+ A small orange taper candle or your wand

TIMING

Day of the week
Tuesday or Sunday

Phase of the moon
Waxing moon

Step one

Lay out the square of fabric and put the butterfly pea flower, horsetail, thuja and cornsilk in the centre. Place the tumbled stone on top of the herbs.

Step two

Take the piece of paper and write down this affirmation: *I am powerful, I am capable, I've got this!*

Fold up the piece of paper and place it on top of the tumbled stone. Then say the affirmation aloud three times, directing your voice towards the contents of the bag.

Step three

Take the corners of the fabric and pull them together to form the bag. Then take the length of cord and use it to secure your bag. Wrap the cord around multiple times and use a sturdy knot to ensure the contents won't fall out.

Step four

If you want to wear your charm bag as a necklace, then measure out enough cord to form a necklace that's a comfortable length for you and tie it off. If you prefer to keep your charm bag in your pocket or handbag, just cut off the cord once it's secure.

Step five

Activate your charm bag by sitting it next to a small orange taper candle and letting it burn down. Alternatively, take your wand and point it at your charm bag. Visualise an aura of orange light around the bag, filling it with the energy of confidence. If you like, play music associated with feeling confident while you do this – maybe 'I Have Confidence' from *The Sound of Music*, or 'I'm Still Standing' by Elton John, or 'Work Bitch' by Britney Spears … whatever works for you.

Step six

Pop your charm bag in your pocket or handbag or hang it around your neck. It's time to step out in style and take the world by storm!

• † •

Angeli vam pomagajo,
da ljubeče govorite svojo resnico.

N°5
CHANEL
PARIS
ELIXIR SENSUEL
SENSUAL ELIXIR

Magic mathematics

Long before the likes of Justin Bieber or One Direction were releasing celebrity fragrances – and who can forget Nicki Minaj's era-defining scent, Minajesty? – the French fashion designer Coco Chanel set the trend with her iconic eau de parfum Chanel No. 5. It's a perfume everybody knows. What a lot of people don't know is the magical significance behind its name.

Coco Chanel was obsessed with numerology, which is the study of the magical meaning and power of numbers. The number 5 was Chanel's lucky number. She had five favourite colours and her first jewellery collection had five themes. She would always hold her fashion shows on 5 February and 5 August. She launched Chanel No. 5 on 5 May 1921 – the fifth day of the fifth month – for maximum good fortune.

Chanel's faith in the number 5 likely traces back to the OG numerologist Pythagoras, an ancient Greek philosopher and mathematician who *really* enjoyed numbers. He believed numbers were the divine building blocks of the cosmos, and that each number had its own spiritual significance. Like Chanel, Pythagoras was a big fan of the number 5, which he saw as the mystical union between masculine and feminine principles. He was also a fan of 1, 2, 3, 4, 6, 7, 8, 9, 10, 27, 28, 35 and 36. Pythagoras would have been a hit on *Sesame Street*.

The ancient Chinese were also big on numbers. Numerology played a major role in fortune-telling, religious rituals, architecture and even daily scheduling. 'Magic squares' were an important aspect of ancient Chinese numerology. A magic square is a square table of numbers in which each row, column and main diagonals always adds up to the same number – kind of like a mystical version of sudoku.

The most renowned magic square was the 'Lo Shu square', which was thought to represent the divine principles of the universe. This is what it looks like:

4	9	2
3	5	7
8	1	6

Whichever way you go, it always adds up to 15!

Magic squares took off in Japan, India and the Islamic world. Eventually they found their way to Renaissance Europe where they became popular with occult practitioners. Magic squares were incorporated into planetary magic (remember planetary hours?). A magic square was assigned to each of the nine planets and their associated powers.

If you want to give planetary magic a go, here's a quick goal-fulfilling spell for you. Just grab an orange piece of paper and draw this magic square on it:

4	14	15	1
9	7	6	12
5	11	10	8
16	2	3	13

This is the 'Jupiter square', so called because Jupiter is a planet associated with success, abundance and generosity. The square adds up to 34.

Once you've drawn the square, take a moment to look at it and imagine a goal you'd like to achieve – career success, home ownership, completing your collection of Sumikko Gurashi plush toys. As they say in bingo, 'Ask for more, it's number 34!'

Once you've finished visualising your goal, set fire to the piece of paper and it's job done! Let the power of numbers work their magic. After all, Chanel No. 5 continues to be the best-selling perfume of all time. If it can work for Coco, it can work for you!

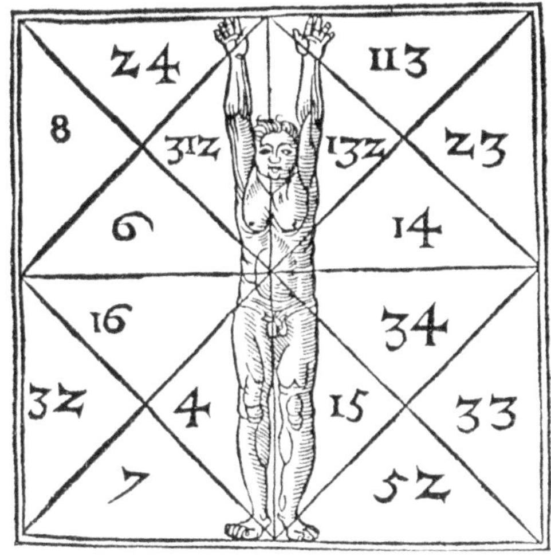

INK
RECORD
Records
Emerald
CITY.
NO R NEILL

PROJECT 13

THE CROWN OF SUCCESS

According to American Puritan folklore, if you wanted to become a witch you had to make a formal pact with the Devil by signing your name in 'the Devil's book' (either in ink or blood, depending on who was telling the story). Once you signed on the dotted line, the Devil would own your soul and you would have magical powers.

Of course, this was just witch-phobic propaganda invented by fun-killing fundamentalists wearing ugly clothes. Nobody ever had to sell their soul to the Devil to become a witch. It's not a thing.

In cultures and communities where magic was an accepted part of life, you usually had to undergo an initiation before you were recognised as a magician, shaman or witch. These rites of passage would typically include a formal ceremony and/or some sort of physical or mental ordeal. As the name suggests, these weren't exactly a walk in the park – we're talking starvation, sleep deprivation, hallucinations, near-death experiences, that sort of thing. Magic wasn't for the faint of heart!

Modern magic has a more relaxed vibe. If you want to identify as a witch, you can just identify as a witch. Job done. You don't have to go through any ritual or ordeal before you start practising magic. You can start anytime you like. Magic is open to everyone.

Even so, initiations remain an important part of modern magic. Initiation ceremonies are still widely practised in magical communities. It's also common for solo practitioners to perform self-initiations. This is the go-to option for people who want to commit to their magical path but don't want to join a community or tradition. Self-initiations often combine traditional techniques with a personal approach, tailor-made to the practitioner's needs. It's magic for the 21st century and we're here for it!

Making ultimate magic

The Crown of Success is the perfect way to take your dark crafting to the next level. You'll use several of the dark crafts we've learned along the way and combine them into a booster-shot of mega-magical power. This self-initiation ceremony will confirm you as a talented master of mystical forces with kick-arse crafting skills! In the eternal words of Glinda, the Good Witch from *The Wizard of Oz*, 'You've always had the power, my dear. You just had to learn it for yourself.'

WHAT YOU'LL NEED

Note: This list doesn't include the ingredients for the other dark crafts included in this spell (ain't nobody got time for that).

+ A large orange tea light candle
+ A handful of dried orange peel
+ Ginger pieces or ginger powder
+ Three drops of ginger oil
+ A dinner plate
+ A square of orange origami paper
+ A pen
+ Matches or a lighter
+ A cauldron (optional)

TIMING

Day of the week
Sunday

Phase of the moon
Full moon

Step one

Take a magical cleansing bath (Project 1). Afterwards, clear your space using your witch's broom or burnables (Project 2). Make sure your space is protected by reactivating your witch jar (Project 4) and putting your devil's trap on display (Project 5). Now you're cleansed, cleared and protected, the crafting can begin!

Step two

Sprinkle the ginger pieces (or ginger powder, or both) on top of the tea candle. Then drip on the ginger oil.

Step three

Draw an image of yourself on one side of the piece of orange origami paper. Don't worry if it's just a stick figure (stick figures can be surprisingly flattering!). Draw yourself in any way that feels right for you.

Step four

Create a sigil (Project 11) using the words 'I AM MAGICAL'. Once the sigil is formed, draw it on the other side of the origami paper.

Step five

Fold up the origami paper and place it in the middle of your plate. Put the tea candle on top of the paper and liberally sprinkle the orange peels around the candle.

Step six

Close your eyes and visualise a crown on your head.

The rim of the crown is made of beautiful wood (the element of earth). The crown is decorated with brightly coloured feathers (the element of air) and studded with aquamarine jewels (the element of water). The points of the crown are five lit orange candles (the element of fire).

Take a moment to enjoy your crown. This is your time to shine!

Step seven

Light the tea candle and hold your hands over it in a blessing gesture. Say this enchantment three times over, louder each time:

In all that I say, and all that I do, success flows through me.

As you say the enchantment, feel the spell's magical power lifting you up, like Beyoncé singing 'Freedom' with Kendrick Lamar at the 2016 BET awards.

Step eight

Circle your wand (Project 3) anticlockwise around the candle seven times to generate energy. Let the candle burn down and set fire to the piece of origami paper. Put the burning origami paper into your cauldron and watch as it burns away.

The Crown of Success is now complete! Congratulations! You've officially graduated from the School of Dark Arts and Crafts! Unlike for a three-day intensive cake-decorating course at your local community centre, you don't get a certificate of completion. But you do get to call on cosmic forces and channel them to your will. On balance, we think you're the winner.

• + •

THE JOURNEY CONTINUES ...

We've reached the end of our dark crafts path. We've covered the four elements, cleansing, protection and activation. We've delved into divination and sympathetic magic. We've sewn poppets, brewed tea, lit candles, drawn sigils and put stuff in bags. We've explored curse tablets, demon traps, the Devil's wedding, donkey's head divination, drumming ghosts, dung magic, emperor-killing immortality elixirs, Enochian wife swaps, a haunted doll island, penises with wings, poisoned love potions and psychedelic witch-brooms. It's been a wild ride.

But as one journey ends, another begins. What we've shown you is only a glimpse of the enchantment that awaits.

Every dark crafter's path is unique. We can't tell you what to do next. We can only encourage you to trust your intuition, get curious, stay respectful and have fun! The good news is that there are lots of fabulous books, websites, podcasts and YouTube videos to help you on your way. Follow the inspiration and see where it takes you. There's a world of spells and sorcery to explore.

We're so excited for all the magic you're going to make!

RECOMMENDED

BOOKS

A History of Magic, Witchcraft and the Occult by DK

Cunningham's Encyclopedia of Magical Herbs by Scott Cunningham

Herbal Tea Magic for the Modern Witch: A Practical Guide to Healing Herbs, Tea Leaf Reading, and Botanical Spells by Elsie Wild

Hidden Paths by Denis Poisson

Hoodoo for Everyone: Modern Approaches to Magic, Conjure, Rootwork, and Liberation by Sherry Shone

Liber Null & Psychonaut: The Practice of Chaos Magic (revised and expanded edition) by Peter J Carroll

Magickal Protection: Defend Against Curses, Gossip, Bullies, Thieves, Demonic Forces, Violence, Threats and Psychic Attack by Damon Brand

Poppet Magick: Patterns, Spells & Formulas for Poppets, Spirit Dolls & Magickal Animals by Silver Ravenwolf

Pure Magic: A Complete Course in Spellcasting by Judika Illes

Sigils, Ciphers and Scripts: The History and Graphic Function of Magick Symbols by MB Jackson

Spell Bound: A New Witch's Guide to Crafting the Future by Chaweon Koo

Sticks, Stones, Roots & Bones: Hoodoo, Mojo & Conjuring with Herbs by Stephanie Rose Bird

The Ancestral Power of Amulets, Talismans, and Mascots: Folk Magic in Witchcraft and Religion by Nigel Pennick

The Crystal Bible (volumes 1, 2 and 3) by Judy Hall

The Complete Book of Incense, Oils and Brews by Scott Cunningham

The Element Encyclopedia of 5000 Spells: The Ultimate Reference Book for the Magical Arts by Judika Illes

The Goodly Spellbook: Olde Spells for Modern Problems by Lady Passion and Diuvei

The Occult, Witchcraft & Magic: An Illustrated History by Christopher Dell

The Witch's Athame: The Craft, Lore, & Magick of Ritual Blades by Jason Mankey

The Witch's Wand: The Craft, Lore, and Magick of Wands & Staffs by Alferian Gwydion MacLir

Traditional Witchcraft: A Cornish Book of Ways by Gemma Gary

Treading the Mill: Workings in Traditional Witchcraft by Nigel Pearson

Weave the Liminal: Living Modern Traditional Witchcraft by Laura Tempest Zakroff

Witchcraft: The Library of Esoterica by Jessica Hundley, Pam Grossman and Thunderwing

PODCASTS

- Glitch Bottle
- Lux Occult
- Mysterious Universe
- New World Witchery – The Search for American Traditional Witchcraft
- Occult of Personality
- Rune Soup
- The History of Witchcraft
- The Lucky Mojo Hoodoo Rootwork Hour
- The Mage's Well
- The Witch Wave

WEBSITES

Haus of Hoodoo hausofhoodoo.com

Morbid Anatomy morbidanatomy.org

Muses of Mystery musesofmystery.com.au

Museum of Witchcraft and Magic museumofwitchcraftandmagic.co.uk

Otherworldly Oracle otherworldlyoracle.com

The Hoodwitch thehoodwitch.com

The Pagan Grimoire pagangrimoire.com

YOUTUBE CHANNELS

Angela's Symposium www.youtube.com/@drangelapuca

Christine McConnell www.youtube.com/@ChristineHMcConnell

Esoterica www.youtube.com/@TheEsotericaChannel

Foolish Fish www.youtube.com/@FoolishFishBooks

Haus of Hoodoo www.youtube.com/@hausofhoodoo293

Practical Peculiarities www.youtube.com/@nikkalcaraz

Religion for Breakfast www.youtube.com/@ReligionForBreakfast

ACKNOWLEDGEMENTS

There were so many magic-makers who brought their touch to this project.

A HUGE thank you to Dana Anderson for her publicity wizardry and getting the book over the line in the first place! What a goddess!

Many thanks to our fabulous publisher Kelly Doust for her invaluable support and guidance. Thanks also to Martin Hughes and Keiran Rogers for believing in us.

Thanks to our amazing editors Elizabeth Robinson-Griffith and Julian Welch for their hard work and thorough checking.

A massive shout out to the whole Affirm Press team for their behind-the-scenes sorcery.

Thanks to Andrew Delaney of Anno Domini Home for his styling flair and letting us use his home to make the photos come to life.

Thanks also to Mic Looby for his sage support and hilarious suggestions during the writing process.

Our eternal gratitude goes to Katie Hilditch for understanding the vision and creating beautiful photos. Our eternal gratitude also goes to Kristy Ford for her incredible design work. You made our book so attractive, alluring and glamorous. Thank you.

Peter would like to thank his dear friends Anna Achia and Denise Parsons for their love and feedback. He'd also like to say 'thank you' and 'I love you' to his husband Mike.

Tehani would like to thank Craig and Maverick for their loving and encouraging support. She'd also like to thank her Grandma Beryl, who taught her about magic and true faeries.

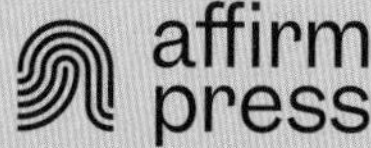

First published by Affirm Press in 2024
Bunurong/Boon Wurrung Country
28 Thistlethwaite Street
South Melbourne VIC 3205
affirmpress.com.au

1 3 5 7 9 10 8 6 4 2

Text copyright © Peter Coleman and Tehani Perham, 2024
All rights reserved. No part of this publication may be reproduced without prior written permission from the publisher.

This work was made on the unceded land of the Bunurong/Boon Wurrung peoples of the Kulin Nation. Affirm Press pays respect to their Elders past and present.

A catalogue record for this book is available from the National Library of Australia

ISBN: 9781922992475 (hardback)

Cover design by Alissa Dinallo © Affirm Press
Internal design by Kristy Ford © Affirm Press
Printed and bound in China by C&C Offset Printing Co.

Every effort has been made to trace copyright holders and to obtain their permission for the use of copyright material. The publisher apologises for any errors or omissions and would be grateful if notified of any corrections that should be incorporated in future editions and reprints of this book.

All internal images are public domain and/or Creative Commons, sourced from Unsplash and Wikimedia Commons. Image on p. 9 by Jitendra Raghuvir, CC BY-SA 4.0 https://creativecommons.org/licenses/by-sa/4.0, via Wikimedia Commons. Image on p. 53 by Wellcome Library, London, CC BY 4.0 https://creativecommons.org/licenses/by/4.0, via Wikimedia Commons. Image on p. 76 by Malcolm Lidbury (aka Pinkpasty), CC BY-SA 3.0 https://creativecommons.org/licenses/by-sa/3.0, via Wikimedia Commons. Image on p. 96 by Wellcome Library, London, CC BY 4.0 https://creativecommons.org/licenses/by/4.0, via Wikimedia Commons